Advance Praise

M000283126

"An expansive, thoughtful synthesis of planning strategies: how they work, when they fail, and why they matter."

Tony Grant, Co-Founder, Sustainable Arts Foundation

"Planning is impossible to perfectly escape or execute. Morville has done a wonderful job of exposing this dilemma without prescribing an outcome."

Josie Barnes Parker, Director, Ann Arbor District Library

"If design and productivity had a baby, this would be the wonderful result. Delightfully punctuated by stories from Peter's life, this guide to planning invites personal reflection while delivering enjoyment and helpful advice."

Richard Dalton, Head of Design, Capital One

"In **Planning for Everything**, Morville shows us that, as designers and strategists, we have the power to truly see the world as it is and imagine how it might be. I was deeply (and wonderfully) challenged to rethink my understanding of goals, planning, and what it means to be fulfilled."

Kristina Halvorson, Founder, Brain Traffic

"It's never been more important to recall that while Eisenhower famously dismissed plans as useless, he firmly believed planning to be indispensable. I'm happy to see Peter bring rigor to this timely and fascinating topic."

Andy Budd, CEO, Clearleft

"Peter has a remarkable gift for making the complex clear. In this book, he shines a light on the murky subject of planning in a way that makes it approachable. As an avid planner myself, I still learned a lot by reading it."

Abby Covert, Information Architect, Etsy

"**Planning for Everything** is a spiritual book in disguise – a meditation on the pivotal roles that intention, attachment, improvisation, iteration, and self-reflection have on the act of design."

Irene Au, Design Partner, Khosla Ventures

"In this delightful book, Peter Morville illuminates the power behind Eisenhower's declaration 'Plans are useless, planning is indispensable.' Peter brings together mindfulness, improvisation, and the observation that the sunk cost theory of perseverance might not be a useful part of our plan. Without prescription or preaching, his conversational tone invites us to reflect on biases, habits, and beliefs that shape our attitudes toward (and thus aptitude for) planning. Chapter by chapter, an informational graphic unfolds to illustrate divergent paths to a goal. Who would have guessed that, far from being a never-ending series of 'to do' tasks, planning can be a divining rod, providing direction and course correction."

Susan Kornfield, Chair, Intellectual Property, Bodman PLC

"Peter Morville has written what will be my personal 'go to' and the first book I recommend to people who hope to model their life (and world) with intent. Practical. Approachable. Wise. This book is a beautiful adventure that will disrupt the way you shape your future."

Priyanka Kakar, User Experience Director, The Walt Disney Company

Planning for Everything

PETER MORVILLE

To Kelly,
Happy Planning!
Peter Morville

SEMANTIC STUDIOS

ANN ARBOR, MICHIGAN

Planning for Everything: The Design of Paths and Goals

by Peter Morville

Semantic Studios

109 Catherine Street

Ann Arbor, Michigan 48104

Web: semanticstudios.com

Email: morville@semanticstudios.com

Editor: Claire Morville

Cover Designers: Jeff Callender and Peter Morville

Interior Designers: Jeff Callender and Peter Morville

Illustrators: Peter Morville and Jeff Callender

© 2018 Peter Morville

All Rights Reserved

ISBN: 978-0-692-05995-1

LCCN: 2018900924

Contents

Preface

"I know why the caged bird sings."
– MAYA ANGELOU

Planning is a skill rarely taught in school. We learn to plan by observation and experience. As we rise from child to teenager, our mastery of the design of paths and goals grows by mighty leaps and bounds; until we stop. It is not a conscious decision. We hit good enough and pivot, as there is so much else to do. It mostly works. We learn to ride a bicycle, and never forget. But planning is different, as it's subject to change. Old habits and beliefs fail as our contexts shift. Happily we can improve, as planning is a skill we can build with practice and wisdom.

I love organizing the future and have been doing it all my life. My parents recall that, as a toddler, I often practiced words in my crib long before going public. And, as a teenager, I drove them crazy on holidays by incessantly asking "what's next?" So it's no surprise I plan software and websites for a living.

But I didn't write this book for me. My aim is to help anyone on the spectrum from playful improviser to rigorous planner to be better at the dance between what is and what might be.

Maya Angelou writes "the caged bird sings of freedom," and I imagine you know what she means. We all feel the cruelty of a cage. Often the bars are hidden. We bind ourselves with laws, code, culture; and fail to see it's a trap. But that's the beauty of the design of paths and goals. By making planning visible, we can improve our ability to find truth and render intent. That's why I wrote this book, because planning is a door to freedom.

Organization of This Book

This book is meant be read in linear style from start to end, but in case you prefer to plan a different way, here's a simple map.

Chapter 1, Realising the Future

Explores the nature of planning in the contexts of animals, people, and robots. Introduces 4 principles and 6 practices.

Chapter 2, Framing

To understand and explain our plans and goals, we must dig deeper into the connections between problems and solutions.

Chapter 3, Imagining

To expand paths and possibilities, play with prototypes. And it helps to have hope, which equals willpower plus waypower.

Chapter 4, Narrowing

To evaluate and filter strategies and options, we identify the drivers, look for levers, and then calculate estimates and risk.

Chapter 5, Deciding

To commit to a belief or goal requires a balance of logic and emotion. Maps and plans help us to shift from why to how.

Chapter 6, Executing

In the improvisational dance of acting and thinking, we must choose to pivot or persist. Grit works but spirit is even better.

Chapter 7, Reflecting

We look back to move forward. We search the past for truths and insights to shift the future. Reflection changes direction.

Chapter 8, Star Finder

Myths shape the future, but do the ends justify the means? In the last chapter, stories of different heroes end with questions.

Acknowledgments

First, I'd like to thank Edgar Schein, as your book on helping inspired my book on planning. Second, I thank Kit Seeborg for your help with the workshop that turned into a book. And, to all 64 people who responded to my survey, thank you for the advice and support I needed to start writing. And, to Rosalind Morville, Christopher Farnum, Heidi Weise, and my friends at Q LTD and The Understanding Group, thanks for standing with me all these years. And, to the folks on my podcast – Jessica Hall, Jorge Arango, Amy Silvers, Rachel Joyce, Peter Merholz, Christina Wodtke, Livia Labate, Tony Grant, Lindsay Kloepping, Martin White, Jonah Bailey, Micah Alles, Jim Young, Jeff Gothelf, Karl Fast, Insa Keilbach – thanks for sharing stories and insights on the design of paths and goals.

Claire Morville and Tony Grant read the draft manuscript and provided generous advice and encouragement. Jeff Callender and I worked together to design the cover, interior layout, and illustrations. All the icons are licensed from The Noun Project.

Finally, I'd like to thank Susan, Claire, and Claudia for making my life worth planning; and Knowsy for our long, slow walks.

Realising the Future

*"One child, one teacher, one book,
one pen can change the world."*
– MALALA YOUSAFZAI

We are several hundred feet into the cave when Claudia whispers in the dark "I'm so mad at you for bringing us here." I'm not surprised. It's my fault. I planned this vacation. I chose to bring my wife and our teenage daughters on this expedition to Actun Tunichil Muknal, a subterranean cave in Belize that contains the sparkling, calcified skeletons of children. Over a thousand years ago, the Maya believed the Cave of the Crystal Sepulchre with its demons, scorpions, and rivers of blood to be an entrance to hell and a fit place for ritual, human sacrifice.

The Maya had a point. After hiking through rainforest in the rain for an hour, swimming an icy stream into the cave mouth, and scrambling over slippery rocks with only headlamps for light, we are cold, tired, fearful. A man sits in the shadows, his face darkened by blood. He must have fallen. That's why our daughter is angry. It's treacherous, and our three hour tour of the underworld has just begun. I'm excited by the wonders of this cave, but I'm also aware of the danger. Since I'm the one who instigated this adventure, I imagine my family may leave me here, a human sacrifice given readily to appease the Gods.

I knew the risks when I planned this holiday. In fact, risk was one of the goals. I asked Susan and the girls what they wanted. We explored options and reflected on past trips. Our teenagers did not want to sit on a beach. They were eager for adventure. So we devised an itinerary to include swimming with sharks, ziplining the jungle, and hiking in caves. I researched hotels, restaurants, transport, things to do. I booked flights, made checklists, and checked passports. I built flexibility into the schedule to allow for weather and mood. I did all of this happily, knowing full well that something would go wrong.

Planning is a skill I love to practice. Whether advising clients how to structure a website, helping teenagers apply to college, or organizing a trip, I love imagining and shaping the future. Not that I have a choice. My brain models possible scenarios obsessively. This is not all good. Yesterday, lost in thought, I walked into a wall. To be in the moment, I must practice mindfulness, which is also essential for planning. Surprise is inevitable. Both the plan and the change need to happen.[1] To manage disruption with grace and a sense of humor is part of the challenge. That's why planning is about more than a plan.

Definitions of Planning

Planning is the design of paths and goals. That's a simple way of describing a complex process that shapes our lives, careers, and dreams more than we realize. It's worthy of study, so let's unravel this humble definition the way we plan: backwards.

Our plans begin with goals. We aim to build a better product, buy a home, survive cancer, throw a party, learn to dance, or teach a class. Of course, it's never that simple. Often we must juggle competing goals with sub-goals and co-goals. In Belize, we want serenity *and* adventure, freedom *and* togetherness, beaches *and* jungles; and our time is limited by commitments at home. Objectives don't exist in isolation. That's what makes planning hard. We must prioritize and make tradeoffs, and to achieve multiple ends, we must carefully choose our means.

All paths are not equal. And, even with a clear goal, it may be true that given one wrong move, you can't get there from here. That's why we imagine steps into strategy in advance. We search for options, model scenarios, estimate risks, and visualize results. There's no one right way, and the shortest path may not be the best. How do we travel from rainforest to beach? We could rent a car, but it's costly, and what if we get lost? How about a bus? It's eco-friendly, and along the way, we may learn about the people and culture of Belize. Our choice of paths is clearly about shaping the future, but it's driven by our beliefs, feelings, and values right here and now.

Figure 1-1. Planning is the design of paths and goals.

Have you ever realised a goal only to realize it didn't deliver what you hoped? Perhaps you bought your first house and regretted it two years later, or got that promotion only to hate your new job. The successful execution of a plan often results in failure, due to faulty mental models in the here and now.

To plan backwards by starting with a goal isn't all wrong, but a satisfying outcome is more likely if we take time to explore the sources of our needs and wants in the past and present. A goal can be a way to channel angst. As Winston Churchill said "Let our advance worrying become our advance thinking and planning."[2] But before we commit to a plan, let's question our feelings and beliefs. Is your fear sensible? Is the path true to your values? Will the plan create the change you want to see? And will that change in the world make you feel what you hope? Plans are built on predictions which are built on beliefs. That's why metacognition – awareness and understanding of one's own thought processes – is essential to good planning.

Of course, it's near as hard to know our own minds as to know the minds of others. Whether we decide to start running, stop smoking, eat less, or study more, we tend to overestimate our ability to stick to the plan. Similarly, when we reach a goal, happiness often fails to endure as expected. We can enhance self-awareness by introspection, but biases and false beliefs are hidden to the mind's eye. That's why planning needs design.

The design of paths and goals invites us to make the invisible visible. A sketch, map, or model helps us think and collaborate by getting the ideas in our heads into the world. While a plan may be defined as a series of steps, planning itself is nonlinear. Diagrams help us see the system. Prototypes let us play with behavior. Together we can find errors and experiment with drivers, levers, metrics, and feedback. By taking the time to make our ideas tangible, we're better able to render our intent.

But we must not be seduced by the artifacts of this process. As Dwight D. Eisenhower warned "plans are useless, planning is indispensable."[3] The truth in this hyperbole is that no plan is perfect, the map is not the territory, surprise is inevitable, we must be prepared to pivot. Planning up front isn't only about making a plan. It's about learning, awareness, and practice; so we can identify options, understand feedback, and deal with disruption. Improvisation favors the prepared mind and body.

The right balance of up front and in process planning depends on context. A software startup in a new market must lean into agility, while a construction firm that builds skyscrapers must commit to blueprints. For both, plans and planning are vital. It's a matter of degree. For our Belize trip, I had a choice. I could have done nothing in advance but book flights, with all places to stay and things to do chosen day to day upon arrival. Some folks love this embrace of serendipity. It can be a lot of fun. In our family, it would create anxiety, so we plan up front while leaving room to respond to weather, mood, and advice.

Ike's famous line on useless plans affords a second insight. No artifact alone can create shared vision. When we plan together, we're able to inspire each other to see and feel what's possible. Leaders can build team loyalty that's tribal. And it's emotional commitment that gives folks the courage and spirit to endure.

Plans are not useless, but they do have their limits, and so do definitions. No statement can fully convey the nature, scope, and meaning of the word it describes. The dictionary defines planning as "the process of making plans." This makes it too easy to see the artifact – the plan – while missing the point.

Figure 1-2. The elements of planning.

In this book, to navigate the design of paths and goals, we'll use a map. The plan is to make planning visible by illumining its elements. But our voyage isn't bound by a fixed course nor divorced from execution. We'll tell stories and take detours in search of divergent views. We shall explore multiple paths on purpose. To understand planning, there's no one right way.

For example, cognitive psychologists have studied the ability to guide action by intention for decades. Together with attention regulation, working memory, impulse control, and empathy, they view planning as an executive function, a core mental process for managing behavior. While researchers struggle with its definition, they mostly agree on its elements.

> The planning process includes at least the following six functions: forming a representation of the problem, choosing a goal, deciding to plan, formulating a plan, executing and monitoring the plan, and learning from the plan.[4]

They recognize that organizing future actions in a complex, uncertain world is difficult and important, noting that planning is the crowning achievement of human cognition. And while they may argue over experimental methods, these scientists all see planning as an ability that can be measured.

One of the most widely used tools to study planning ability is the Tower of Hanoi. This ancient puzzle consists of three pegs and a set of rings of varied sizes that can slide onto any peg. The game starts with all rings on one peg stacked neatly from biggest at the bottom to smallest on top. The goal is to move the stack to a new peg while following the rules: you may only move one ring at a time, a move consists of placing the upper ring from one peg on top of another, no ring can be put atop a smaller ring. A game with three rings requires a minimum of seven moves, but play with five rings and it takes thirty one.

The puzzle tests our ability to organize a sequence of actions. Players may be evaluated by completion time and number of moves. Since it's costly to backtrack, it helps to plan ahead by simulating moves in the mind. Of course, some folks are better at this task than others, and that's the point of the experiment.

Unsurprisingly, age plays a role. Most three and four year olds are unable to solve the puzzle with three rings. Success rates rise dramatically in the 7-9 and 11-14 age ranges, then fall gradually as we transition from adulthood to old age. Health is also a factor. People with Alzheimer's, Parkinson's, or attention deficit hyperactivity disorder often struggle with these tests. Beyond the obvious, it's hard to identify what influences our ability to plan. Children in low income families tend to be poor at planning, and this correlates with academic success, but there are too many variables to declare causality. Studies show the relation of planning skills to IQ is moderate at best. So why do we differ so widely in our ability to plan?

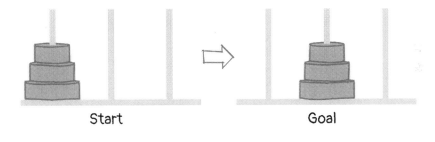

Start   Goal

Figure 1-3. Tower of Hanoi.

The answer lies partly in our personal biases towards initial or concurrent planning. In a Tower of Hanoi study, pre-planners performed best in the three and four ring games, but those who declined to plan up front were best at the five ring game. Apparently, initial planners gain an advantage by simulating moves, but their minds can handle only so much complexity. But that doesn't explain why low initial planners outperform high initial planners in games requiring 15 or more moves. In analyzing the data, which included verbal statements by participants, the researchers made an intriguing observation.

Those who tend to plan extensively before attempting the solution to a problem also tend to plan much less as they solve the problem. In contrast, those who do not plan in an initial preparation phase tend to plan concurrently as they solve the problem.[5]

In short, it's not a matter of whether but when we plan, and our habits may help or hinder based on the context. There's another piece to this puzzle worth grasping. It's hard to imagine and solve the Tower of Hanoi in your mind. And while a picture helps, it's no substitute for the puzzle itself. To see, touch, and move wooden rings makes a huge difference.

Interestingly, the pieces need not be physical. If you've ever played Tetris, you know that to succeed at this tile matching video game, it's vital to think-spin concurrently. Novices tend to rotate falling *zoids* in their minds before rotating them in the game, but in time players learn digital spins are faster. Studies show manual rotation to be as quick as 150 microseconds, whereas mental rotation takes five to ten times longer.[6] So novices plan and then act, whereas experts act-plan together.

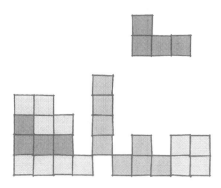

Figure 1-4. In Tetris, experts spin-think concurrently.

It's an illustration of embodied cognition and extended mind. To think and plan, we use bodies, tools, and environments; not just our brains. Consider the goal of making a hot breakfast of eggs, bacon, toast, and coffee. What are the steps? What are the risks and tradeoffs? How might you organize your tools, ingredients, and physical space? How is your plan shaped by your body? Will you be relying on your eyes, ears, and nose?

Using puzzles and games to study planning in the lab enables scientists to control the variables, but it does so at the expense of ecological validity. In the real world, even daily tasks such as cooking and shopping are complex. A study can measure path efficiency, but it's not feasible to account for all the risks and tradeoffs inherent in planning a trip to the grocery store. When should you go? Which route will you take? Does the car need gas? Do you make a list? Do you need milk? Do you call your spouse to find out? What if you run into *that* person?

It's not feasible to list all the questions, as the mix of desires and anxieties we bring to the task is idiosyncratic. And, once in the store, our plans may change. What we see, hear, smell, and taste may make us buy on impulse. How we feel affects our planning and behavior. The variables are out of control. Planning is an art that can't be contained by science.

However, an insight we can draw with confidence from the body of scientific research is that we can get better at planning. Countless studies have charted the development of planful behavior from infancy into adolescence. In one 1980s survey, children were asked "what kinds of things are planned?" For 5-year olds, top responses included recurrent daily actions and searching for lost items, while the 7-year olds planned to avoid commitments and manipulate grownups.[7] The top response of 11-year olds was relations with peers. In the same study, when asked "what's difficult about planning?" the 11-year olds cited memory and information gathering, whereas most 5-year olds answered "nothing." Clearly the Dunning-Kruger effect – the cognitive bias that renders people unable to realize their own incompetence – applies to planning. The good news is that for most of us self-awareness and planning skills improve as we mature. The better news is that we can speed up this process.

A substantial body of evidence suggests that planning abilities can be enhanced by education and experience. In particular, exercises in *planning together* help people get better at problem solving, decision making, and metacognition. When we share responsibility for planning, we share strategies, insights, tools, and tactics that improve our ability to design paths and goals.

These findings aren't just academic. For instance, research by the U.S. Marine Corps revealed "the most successful Marines were those with a strong *internal locus of control* – a belief they could influence their destiny through the choices they made."[8] An internal locus of control is linked to self-motivation, social maturity, professional success, happiness, and a longer life.

It's also vital to a Marine since no plan survives contact with the enemy. In the field, a Marine must adapt plans to reconcile changing conditions with commander's intent. It may not be possible to follow orders. For this reason, the Marine Corps encourages a growth mindset and builds planning skills. And it works. Studies show "the average recruit's internal locus of control increases significantly during basic training."[9] Or in the words of J.D. Vance who credits the Marines with saving his life "I left the Marine Corps not just with a sense that I could do what I wanted but also with the capacity to plan."[10]

If you'd prefer to bring discipline to planning without the danger of mortal combat, David Allen has the system for you. His book *Getting Things Done* defines a five-step process to master workflow and get control of your life.[11] First, capture (1) what has your attention. Write down everything you must do. Get ideas out of your head and into your inbox right away, so you can rely on recognition, not recall. Then, clarify (2) the nature of each item. Is it actionable? Is it part of a project? And what's the immediate "next action" that must occur?

Next, organize (3) the results into eight categories (*projects, project plans, waiting, calendar, next actions, someday/maybe, trash, reference*). Then, reflect (4) on your task list and schedule. Use a weekly review to step back and see the whole picture. Finally, engage (5) by trusting your intuition to make decisions in the moment about what to do. Now you're getting things done!

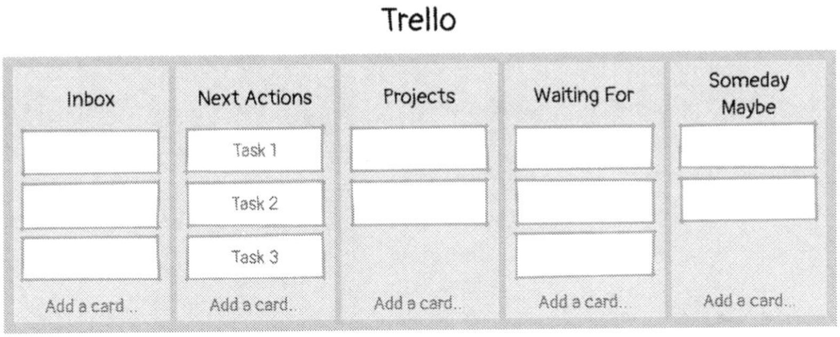

Trello

Inbox	Next Actions	Projects	Waiting For	Someday Maybe
	Task 1			
	Task 2			
	Task 3			
Add a card..	Add a card.	Add a card.	Add a card.	Add a card.

Figure 1-5. Getting Things Done in Trello.

It's a good system. The book is a bestseller and has inspired an industry of apps including OmniFocus, Evernote, and Trello. In fact, GTD is so popular, some folks call it a cult. While I'm not sure that's fair, it does raise a concern. GTD is prescriptive and details a process that's one size fits all. My aim with this book is the opposite. I plan to describe and illustrate diverse ways of planning, so you may decide what works best for you.

GTD's definition of planning as the path to productivity isn't wrong. But it is narrow. We should not limit ourselves to efficiency metrics when it comes to organizing the future. We must embrace a more expansive definition, and towards that end, I submit **nine theses** about the design of paths and goals.

Planning is impossible and essential. We can't predict the future in a complex, uncertain world, yet we do it all the time. We plan our days, weeks, projects, meetings, vacations, births, marriages, careers, and retirements. Often, as we hate uncertainty, we ignore it, then learn the hard way even the best laid plans are subject to disruption. Some try not to plan, but that's like trying not to think. Iterative, incremental planning makes sense when we must act to understand, but even an agile process is a plan.

Planning is a skill. This means we can get better. Infants barely plan. As our minds and bodies develop, so does our capacity to plan. Some kids have more interest and aptitude than others. Some have better teachers. Our skills are shaped by interaction with our parents, peers, culture, and environment. As we mature, the way we plan becomes a habit. We plan without thinking about how we plan. We get things done efficiently but miss opportunities that go unseen. Fortunately, since planning is a skill, people of any age or ability can grow their literacy by learning and practicing.

Planning creates possibility. We spend most of our lives on autopilot. Our ways of acting and seeing are deeply ingrained. Planning opens the door to change. If we're willing to break old habits and try new ways of planning, we may discover better paths and goals. Planning is an invisible lever that can move the world.

Plans are built on beliefs. To understand and navigate a complex world, we digest our experiences into models and beliefs. Plans are built on top. But as the map is not the territory, our predictions go awry. In search of truth, we must use information, experiments, and metrics wisely. To see clearly, it helps to go meta. By being mindful, we can identify gaps, adjust maps, and build better plans.

Strategies are built on options. There's no strategy without choice, and no choice without awareness of options. Before defining a path to a goal, it's vital to expand our understanding of possible steps and sequences. How might we see what we're missing? Who can help? What if we reimagine the project as a process? Good strategy means asking the right questions and becoming aware of options.

There is no one right way. We may begin with research, strategy, and design, but that's not the only way. Sometimes it's best to act first. A minimum viable product can be the fastest way to learn. A prescription may be the safest path to diagnosis. Our methods must fit the context, leverage our strengths, and realise our goals and values. To this end, we can learn from architects, executives, artists, teachers, athletes, activists; and the list goes on. Planning is enhanced by diversity, because there are many good ways to plan.

We must use experts wisely. There's value in specialized expertise, education, and experience. There's simply no substitute for the skill and wisdom of those who have been there and done that within a particular context. On the other hand, experts are subject to bias and perverse incentives. Ideally, your expert has skin in the game. It's easier to trust pilots than doctors. Either way, ask them to map the plan, and to be explicit about options, risks, metrics, and goals. Seek to understand, demand agency, and never follow blindly.

We can plan a better future. These are the best and worst of times in which to plan, for disruption holds promise and peril, people and technology are imperfect, artificial intelligence is no substitute for intelligence augmentation, and the only way out is through. In an era of drones and demagogues, we can't get by on autopilot. So let's disrupt ourselves by changing how we plan. Imagining a light at the end of the tunnel is the first step out of the dark.

Planning can be fun. If you hate planning, you're doing it wrong. Plan with a friend, make a map, embrace uncertainty, daydream, and go for a walk. Our ability to imagine, organize, and invent the future is a gift. Shift procrastination into playing with planning.

These theses are intended as definitions, provocations, and invitations to reflect. What do you think? Are there ideas that make you frown or smile and nod your head? Either way I'm happy as your consent is not my goal. This book isn't designed to transfer knowledge. I can't tell you how to plan. But maybe we can figure it out together. My mindset is conversational. In sharing my ideas, I invite you to question yours. And I hope to hear back. What did you learn? What did I miss? Only you can discover the paths and goals that work for you. The meaning of planning depends on purpose, preference, and context. So let's go beyond definitions to look at who plans and why.

Systems and Contexts

Imagine you're scuba diving in the Caribbean when you spy an octopus tip-toeing across the sandy seabed while carrying two halves of a coconut. How do you explain what you see? As a nurse shark glides into the picture, the octopus pulls the shells together and hides inside the coconut. What's up? Is it instinct? Can an octopus plan ahead? What do you believe?

René Descartes, the philosopher, mathematician, and scientist who crowed *I think, therefore I am* defined animals as automata, machines without minds or souls, brutes incapable of thought. Two hundred years later, William Hazlitt, a British writer and philosopher, continued to mine the same (vain) vein.

> Man is the only animal that laughs and weeps; for he is the only animal that is struck with the difference between what things are, and what they ought to be.[12]

Is man the only animal that thinks about the future? Before answering, note that octopuses do indeed carry coconuts. There's video on YouTube. Author of *The Soul of an Octopus,* Sy Montgomery believes these spirited creatures know exactly what they're doing, explaining "octopuses are well aware of their vulnerability and make plans to protect themselves."[13]

And, in exhibiting planful behavior, the octopus is far from alone. Wild chimps carry toolkits of up to five different sticks and twigs to hunt for ants and raid bees' nests for honey. Ants that find liquefied food such as rotting fruit leave and return with sand grains or soft wood to soak up the juice so they can carry it back to the nest. Elephants use logs to flatten electric fences, make tools to remove ticks and scratch backs, and survive droughts by walking hundreds of miles along routes and to water sources they've not used for decades.[14] Even our dog Knowsy makes plans. She finds her throw toy and drops it at our feet so we will play with her. And she barks to go out, so she can bark to come in, so she can bark for her dinner.

These examples ask us to question not only the intelligence of animals but also the nature of planning. For instance, consider the elephants who travel in bond groups made of two or more families, usually led by the oldest female. The matriarch decides where to go and when. To lead well, she must recall the locations of food and water, consider the capabilities of family members, and overcome such obstacles as electric fences. Her ability to draw on memory, empathy, and insight for planning is inspiring, and it's why elephants live longer when led by matriarchs over thirty five. Wisdom takes time.

Traditionally, humans have captured our wisdom in stories and myths. Notably *The Ants and the Grasshopper* by Aesop uses caricatures of animals to convey a lesson about planning.

> On a cold, frosty day the ants began dragging out some of the grain they had stored during the summer and began drying it. A grasshopper, half-dead with hunger, came by and asked for a morsel to save his life. "What did you do this past summer?" responded the ants. "Oh," said the grasshopper, "I kept myself busy by singing all day long and all night too." "Well then," remarked the ants, as they laughed and shut their storehouse, "since you kept yourself busy by singing all summer, you can do the same by dancing all winter."

The moral of the story which we tell to our children is as hard as it is simple: plan or die. It's a truth of nature and society. In the ecosystems of nature, planning is an emergent property of organisms subjected to natural selection. And in our system of civilization, planning is a core life skill for people subjected to capitalism. For all animals, including homo sapiens, the root cause of planning is survival. But do we plan only to pass on genes? Are our goals defined by the need to spread DNA? Or are our quests also about meaning, curiosity, love, and hope?

What about the elephants? Are they so different? Do we seriously believe they can design and execute complex plans without mental models or an ability to think about the future? And when we see a mother elephant rescue her screaming baby who got himself stuck in a water hole, can we really deny their sentience? I think not. I feel, therefore I am. Not only does Descartes' framing of animals as objects not subjects run counter to common sense; it's unsupported by science as illustrated by the 2012 *Cambridge Declaration on Consciousness*.

> The weight of evidence indicates that humans are not unique in possessing the neurological substrates that generate consciousness. Non-human animals, including all mammals and birds, and many other creatures including octopuses also possess these substrates.[15]

Similarly, the evidence suggests that feelings – which may lead us to fall in love, fight a war, write a song, code software, or eat chocolate ice cream – are not at all unique to humans.

> Hormones and neurotransmitters, the chemicals associated with human desire, fear, love, joy, and sadness are highly conserved across taxa. This means that whether you're a person or a monkey, a bird or a turtle, an octopus or a clam, the physiological changes that accompany our deepest felt emotions appear to be the same.[16]

Emotions are more important to planning than we know. This is why it often makes sense to trust your gut. But it's also why we must be wary of politicians and philosophers. The hidden lesson in the myth that animals aren't sentient is that humans have a remarkable ability to believe what we want. Descartes' denial enabled guilt-free animal research and factory farming; and followed in the footsteps of Aristotle's *great chain of being* which placed man atop the taxonomy as the only animal with a rational soul. We humans want to be good and feel special, so we're easily seduced by exceptionalism. Mark Twain poked fun at this habit, noting "Man is the only animal that blushes, or needs to."[17] While self-soothing is a survival skill, our feel-good beliefs blind us to the truth and affect our ability to plan.

For instance, our beliefs about human singularity, intelligence, and planning led to failure (and blushing) during the early years of artificial intelligence and robotics. The quest to create AI was launched in 1955 with more than a dash of hubris.

> An attempt will be made to find how to make machines use language, form abstractions and concepts, solve problems now reserved for humans, and improve themselves. We think that a significant advance can be made in one or more of these areas if a carefully selected group of scientists work together for a summer.[18]

To these scientists, it was obvious that the brain is a computer, and the computer is a brain, so it made sense to use top-down models to leap directly to rational, disembodied intelligence. In 1965 Herbert Simon claimed "Machines will be capable within twenty years of doing any work a man can do,"[19] and Marvin Minsky upped the ante in 1970 by predicting that "in three to eight years we will have a machine with the general intelligence of an average human being."[20] Needless to say, this didn't occur, and the field faced cutbacks and criticism.

In Greek mythology, hubris reliably leads to nemesis. Icarus drowned in the sea after flying too close to the sun. And in the Bible, pride goeth before a fall. Pride is the original and most serious of the seven deadly sins. So, with respect to the field's proud pioneers, you might say their shame was predictable.

During the winters of AI, a second way to intelligence took root. Lucy Suchman compared the two paths in her 1987 book *Plans and Situated Actions* which begins with this quote.

> Thomas Gladwin has written a brilliant article contrasting the method by which the Trukese navigate the open sea, with that by which Europeans navigate. He points out that the European navigator begins with a plan – a course – which he has charted according to certain universal principles, and he carries out his voyage by relating his every move to that plan. His effort throughout is directed to remaining "on course." If unexpected events occur he must first alter the plan, then respond accordingly.

The Trukese navigator begins with an objective rather than a plan. He sets off toward the objective and responds to conditions as they arise in an ad hoc fashion. He utilizes information provided by the wind, the waves, the tide and current, the fauna, the stars, the clouds, the sound of the water on the side of the boat, and he steers accordingly. His effort is directed to doing whatever is necessary to reach that objective. If asked, he can point to his objective at any moment, but he cannot describe his course.[21]

Lucy noted our culture favors abstract, analytic thinking and actions determined by plans; and that this mindset was "being reified in the design of intelligent machines."[22] The problem in her words is that "stated in advance, plans are necessarily vague,"[23] and that ad hoc situated action is how we thrive in a complex, unpredictable world. She understood that to build robots able to act and interact in the real world, we must focus less on abstract rationality and more on embodied interaction.

This view was shared by Rodney Brooks who in 1987 argued for an evolutionary approach based on perception and action.

It is instructive to reflect on the way in which earth-based biological evolution spent its time. Single-cell entities arose out of the primordial soup roughly 3.5 billion years ago. A billion years passed before photosynthetic plants appeared. After almost another billion and a half years, around 550 million years ago, the first fish and vertebrates arrived, and insects 450 million years ago. Then things started moving fast. Reptiles arrived 370 million years ago, followed by dinosaurs at 330 and mammals at 250 million years ago. The first primates appeared 120 million years ago and the immediate predecessors to the great apes 18 million years ago. Man arrived in roughly his present form 2.5 million years ago. He invented agriculture a mere 19,000 years ago, writing less than 5,000 years ago, and "expert" knowledge only over the last few hundred years. This suggests that problem solving behavior, language, expert knowledge and application, and reason are all pretty simple once the essence of being and reacting are available.[24]

Rodney saw abstraction as the essence of intelligence and realized in the real world, there's no clean division between perception (abstraction) and reasoning. He saw intelligence must be built bottom-up, not top-down. In a nod to his peers, he noted talk is cheap, defined his goal, and got to work.

> I wish to build completely autonomous mobile agents that co-exist in the world with humans, and are seen by humans as intelligent beings in their own right. I will call such agents Creatures.[25]

Rodney insisted that a Creature must be able to pursue multiple goals, adapt to changes in its environment, and have a purpose. So, like an insect or a Trukese navigator, a Creature is an intelligent agent driven by an objective, not a fixed plan.

In pursuit of his goal, Rodney co-founded iRobot and to the delight of cats around the world, created the first successful, domestic robot, Roomba. These vacuums don't map rooms but rely on sensors and algorithms such as spiral cleaning, room crossing, wall following, and random walk angle changing after bumping into an object. Their unplanned paths aren't efficient, but they are adaptive and surprisingly effective.

Recently we've seen progress in machine learning, a branch of AI focused on agents that learn by finding patterns in data. In 1996 when Deep Blue beat chess champion Garry Kasparov by studying 200 million positions per second, it was a display of raw computing power. But when AlphaGo beat Lee Seedol in 2016, it was because Google found a way to Go bottom-up.

> The search space in Go is vast, more than a googol times larger than chess, a number greater than there are atoms in the universe. As a result, traditional brute force AI methods which construct a search tree of all possible sequences of moves don't have a chance.

> We first trained the policy network on 30 million moves from games played by human experts, until it could predict the human move 57% of the time. But our goal was to beat the best human players, not just mimic them. To do this, AlphaGo learned to discover new strategies for itself, by playing thousands of games between its neural networks, and gradually improving them using a trial-and-error process known as reinforcement learning.[26]

In short, AlphaGo acts on predictions based on experience and imagination, much like an elephant or a human. And it's one of several technologies along with chatbots, humanoid robots, and self-driving cars that are putting the hype back into AI. In a recent survey of artificial intelligence researchers, the experts agreed there is a 50% chance of AI outperforming humans in all tasks in 45 years and of automating all human jobs in 120 years.[27] And then there's *Skynet*. Public fear of the existential risk posed by a superintelligent AI is on the rise. Elon Musk, Stephen Hawking, and Bill Gates have issued dire warnings.

But Rodney Brooks argues we're repeating our prideful errors by overestimating our understanding of consciousness.

> The worry stems from a fundamental error in not distinguishing between the very real recent advances in a particular aspect of AI and the enormity and complexity of building sentient volitional intelligence…deep learning does not help in giving a machine intent or any overarching goals or wants.[28]

Based on decades of experience building autonomous, mobile Creatures, Rodney tells us to relax and suggests that if we're spectacularly lucky over the next thirty years, we'll have AI with the intentionality of a lizard. Machines excel at prediction and the optimization of paths, but they are artless in the design of goals. So, is the Singularity imminent, or is it a goofy hypothesis built on false beliefs? Will truck drivers be out of work in a decade? How about surgeons? Is medical school a dead end? I'm not sure what to believe. As Yogi Berra opined "it's tough to make predictions, especially about the future."[29]

But we don't have a choice. Plans are built on predictions which are built on beliefs, and planning is what we do. As human beings with free will, we can't not plan. And I'm not just talking about trips to Belize. We plan for everything. As computer and neuroscience pioneer Jeff Hawkins explains, planning is deeper and more pervasive than we may think.

Our brains use stored memories to constantly make predictions about everything we see, feel, and hear. When I look around the room, my brain is using memories to form predictions about what it expects to experience before I experience it…Prediction is not just one of the things your brain does. It is the primary function of the neocortex, and the foundation of intelligence.[30]

When you open a door, and it works the way you predict, you don't think about or recall it. But if a door is stuck or a knob falls off, expectations are violated, you pay attention, a new memory is made, and predictions are adjusted. Prospection, the ability to imagine and evaluate possible futures, is so core to being human that Martin Seligman argues our species should be renamed from Homo Sapiens to Homo Prospectus.

What if perception is less about the registration of what is present, than about generating a reliable hallucination of what to expect? What if memory is not a drawer of photographs, but a changing collection of possibilities? What if emotion is not agitation from the now, but guidance for the future? What if happiness is not the report of a current state, but the prediction of how things are going to go? What if we are not Homo Sapiens, but Homo Prospectus?[31]

To understand this perspective, it's helpful to consider our two systems of thought.[32] System 1 is intuitive, emotional, fast, automatic, and biased by data and heuristics. System 2 is conscious, logical, deliberate, and likes to think it's in charge. Beliefs and actions arise from these systems' interaction. With this model in mind, Seligman describes two kinds of emotion.

Full-blown emotion is what people ordinarily understand by the term emotion. It is a state of conscious feeling, typically marked by bodily changes such as breathing fast, elevated heartbeat, maybe flushing, and even tears. It is felt as a single state. It arises slowly and dissipates slowly too. In contrast, automatic affect is simply a twinge of feeling that something is good or bad. It is typically automatic and may be entirely unconscious.[33]

The goal of full-blown emotion is to get our attention, cause reflection, and stimulate learning, whereas twinges help us judge whether a plan is good or bad. Consider, for instance, a man who commits an immoral act, then feels full-blown guilt. He reflects on his conduct and imagines how he might have acted differently. The next time he's tempted, he feels a twinge of anticipatory guilt, and chooses a different path. In this way, the twinge guides action and avoids the full-blown emotion.

We experience full-blown anger, fear, sadness, and happiness infrequently, but we feel twinges every day, often in response to reality but also triggered by our thoughts. Studies show that mind wandering occurs in adults nearly 50% of the time.[34] As we reflect on recent paths and wonder about future goals, these twinges inform our mental models and shape our plans. We also distill life into abstractions and explanations as we sleep. A dream that wanders beyond a twinge is a nightmare.

A few years ago, I solo hiked the Grand Canyon, from the South Rim to the North Rim in a day.[35] As I wandered the desert scrub beyond Phantom Ranch, I was thinking deep thoughts about two thousand million year old rocks. They made me feel small. While we're more stable than a tornado or a sandbar, we belong in the same category. We are delicate, imperfect patterns that come and go in the blink of an eye. But we are also more ancient than rocks. We're made of stardust, indestructible matter as old as the universe. That's when I heard the rattle. Lost in thought, I nearly stepped on a snake.

A while later, as the full-blown fear subsided, my curiosity about rattlesnakes grew. After noting the obvious – that the purpose of the rattle is to avoid conflict – I was saddened by reports they may be silenced by evolution. Those that rattle are killed by humans, so rattlesnakes increasingly don't. Now I'm torn. System 2 has convinced a part of me to feel protective towards rattlesnakes, while System 1 warns me with fear. I have no practical need to overcome this prejudice, but if I did, I know safe exposure would be the best plan. Logic alone would fail. System 2 is no match for System 1. But if I spent time with snakes without being hurt, my fear would abate. With respect to rattlesnakes, I'm not sure that's what I want.

But not all our instincts and learned biases are good. To the contrary, we live in a society that suffers from racism, sexism, and other types of bigotry. So it helps to know how to teach your gut. It can't be done solely with facts, figures, and logic, and it can't be done fast. System 1 learns like the machine that plays Go. It needs sufficient data to identify patterns to shape predictions to change behavior. Today's undergraduates grew up in a world in which LGBTQ+ people were more visible. As a result they're more aware of and less threatened by diversity than previous generations.[36] Experience can override defaults.

You may fear that mind wandering has taken us off topic, but belief lies at the heart of planning. Belief is a hidden force that shapes both paths and goals. If we ignore the sources of intent and prediction in others and in ourselves, our plans are sure to fail. And if we're blind to bias in how we plan, we're likely to miss alternatives. As individuals, we're all on the spectrum in our planning defaults, bounded by control freaks wedded to upfront plans and disruptive improvisers who move fast and break things. And that's okay. It often makes sense to admit our preferences and play to our strengths. But not always. In some contexts, defaults are simply faults. We see this all the time in the unpredictable ecosystems we call organizations.

Starting a job is one of life's major stressors, in part because we must discover and adapt to idiosyncratic ways of thinking and doing embedded as organizational culture. At first, we try to fit in by wearing the right clothes, but deeper changes in our beliefs, values, and habits are often required to truly belong. In particular, a practice we may need to shift is planning. The way an organization designs goals and paths is at the heart of its culture. If your default is different, it will create friction.

To understand planning in an organizational context, it helps to know history, since the past is buried in the present. Until recently, workers used common sense and rule of thumb, but in the late 1800s and early 1900s, Frederick Taylor introduced "scientific management" and radically changed how we plan.

Taylor studied steel workers and sought to apply engineering principles to work on the factory floor. In pursuit of efficiency and productivity, he pioneered time and motion studies, and the division of roles and responsibilities into precisely defined tasks. A hero of the industrial age, he wrote "In the past the man has been first; in the future the system must be first."[37]

Taylor was consumed with finding the "one best way," and as Peter Drucker noted in 1974, he made an enduring impact.

> Frederick W. Taylor was the first man in recorded history who deemed work deserving of systematic observation and study. On Taylor's scientific management rests, above all, the tremendous surge of affluence in the last seventy-five years which has lifted the working masses in the developed countries well above any level recorded before, even for the well-to-do.[38]

His biographer explains that Taylor called for the "complete handover of all planning, control, and decision making from the workmen to the new class of scientific managers,"[39] and in this industrial era solution lies an information age problem.

Times of rapid change and increasing complexity require a shift from optimization towards innovation. Forcing workers to blindly execute the upfront plans and sequential processes of the "waterfall model" turns out *not* to be the one best way.

But we do it anyway. Taylor's obsession with time, order, and efficiency has been absorbed into the fabric of our culture. We share his faith in reductionism. We divide projects into phases into tasks. We separate people into teams into roles. We split work into steps and silos. Then things fall through the cracks.

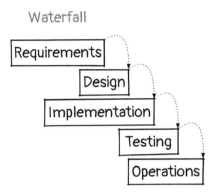

Figure 1-6. The Waterfall Model.

It's not that waterfall is wrong. In many contexts, it's a useful model. The problem is that, all too often, we apply it without realizing it's not the only way. Again, it helps to know history.

In the 1950s, Toyota figured out how to avoid the pitfalls of Taylorism by embracing what's now called Lean. In design, all relevant specialists were involved at the outset, so conflicts about resources and priorities were resolved early on. And in production, managers learned that by making small batches and giving every worker the ability to stop the line, they could identify, fix, and prevent errors more quickly and effectively.[40]

Rather than serving as cogs in the machine, workers were expected to solve problems by using "the five why's" to systematically trace every error to its root cause. Similarly, suppliers were expected to coordinate the flow of parts and information within the just-in-time supply system of kanban.

This radical transparency ensured that everyone knew a missing part could stop the whole system. Managers gave workers and suppliers an unprecedented level of information and responsibility, so they could contribute to continuous, incremental planning and improvement. And it worked.

Quality soared, and Toyota became the largest, most consistently successful industrial enterprise in the world.

In recent years, Eric Ries famously adapted Lean to solve the wicked problem of software startups: what if we build something nobody wants?[41] He advocates use of a minimum viable product ("MVP") as the hub of a Build-Measure-Learn loop that allows for the least expensive experiment. By selling an early version of a product or feature, we can get feedback from customers, not just about how it's designed, but about what the market actually wants. Lean helps us find the goal.

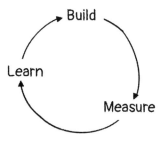

Figure 1-7. The Lean Model.

Agile is a similar mindset that arose in response to frustration with the waterfall model in software development. Agilistas argue that while Big Design Up Front may be required in the contexts of manufacturing and construction where it's costly if not impossible to make changes during or after execution, it makes no sense for software. Since requirements often change and code can be edited, the *Agile Manifesto* endorses flexibility.

Individuals and interactions over processes and tools.

Working software over comprehensive documentation.

Customer collaboration over contract negotiation.

Responding to change over following a plan.

The rapid, widespread adoption of agile methodologies such as Scrum has provided a much needed shift in business from fixed to flexible mindsets. Of course, the original principles are often misunderstood or taken too far. Notably, Agile is seen as a license to make it up as we go. The authors of the manifesto explain "while there is value in the items on the right, we value the items on the left more," but their nod to balance is subtle and easily missed. Fortunately, the folks behind the most successful agile methodologies were paying attention.

> One of the most common myths of agile software development is that agile teams don't plan. In fact, agile teams do a much more thorough job of planning than many traditional project teams.[42]

The practices and artifacts of Scrum – backlogs, sprints, stand ups, increments, burn charts – reflect an understanding of the need to strike a balance between planning and improvisation, and the value of engaging the entire team in both. As we'll see later, Agile and Lean ideas can be useful beyond their original ecosystems, but translation must be done mindfully.

The history of planning from Taylor to Agile reflects a shift in the zeitgeist – the spirit of the age – from manufacturing to software that affects all aspects of work and life. In business strategy, attention has shifted from formal strategic planning to more collaborative, agile methods. In part, this is due to the clear weakness of static plans as noted by Henry Mintzberg.

> Plans by their very nature are designed to promote inflexibility. They are meant to establish clear direction, to impose stability on an organization…planning is built around the categories that already exist in the organization.[43]

But the resistance to plans is also fueled by fashion. In many organizations, the aversion to anything old is palpable. Project managers have burned their Gantt charts. Everything happens emergently in Trello and Slack. And this is not all good. As the pendulum swings out of control, chaos inevitably strikes. In organizations of all shapes and sizes, the failure to fit process to context hurts people and bottom lines. It's time to realize we can't not plan, and there is no one best way. Defining and embracing a process *is* planning, and it's vital to find your fit.

That's why I believe in planning by design. As a professional practice, design exists across contexts. People design all sorts of objects, systems, services, and experiences. While each type of design has unique tools and methods, the creative process is inspired by commonalities. Designers make ideas tangible so we can see what we think. And as Steve Jobs noted, "It's not just what it looks like and feels like. Design is how it works."[44]

So before working to design the thing right, we must first be sure we're designing the right thing. This calls for a process of diverging and converging twice. The "Double Diamond" asks us to discover many possible paths and goals before we define the problem and craft the plan; and then to develop and test prototypes before deciding upon and delivering the solution.[45]

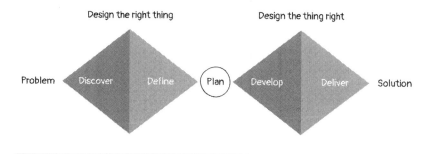

Figure 1-8. The Double Diamond.

At the heart of design is our ability to model the world as it is and as it might be. This is powerful. A sketch or prototype can spark insights and change minds. Goals and vision may shift in a "now that I see it" moment. In recent years, business has begun to adapt these practices to strategy and planning under the aegis of Design Thinking. Post-its and prototypes engage our brains, bodies, colleagues, customers, and ecosystems in distributed cognition. Design helps us solve wicked problems by exploring paths and goals. And it works for individuals and teams, not just big business. In short, design is a great fit for planning, and its practices are the inspiration for this book.

Principles and Practices

The discovery of planful behavior in animals, robots, people, and organizations reveals that planning is a big, messy subject. As we shift from introductory definitions into the book's core practical chapters, we'll focus on planning for people. The aim is to help individuals and teams get better at the design of paths and goals. The plan is to build understanding, skills, and literacy by studying four principles and six practices.

Figure 1-9. Four principles.

To serve memory and use, I've arranged these principles and practices into a mnemonic – STAR FINDER. In astronomy, a "star finder" or planisphere is a map of the night sky used for learning to identify stars and constellations. In this book, it's a guide for finding goals, finding paths, and finding your way.

First, we can get better at planning by making planning more social, tangible, agile, and reflective. At each step in the design of paths and goals, ask how these four principles might help.

Social. Plan with people early and often. Engage family, friends, colleagues, customers, stakeholders, and mentors in the process. When we plan together, it's easier to get started. Also, diversity grows empathy, sharing creates buy-in, and both expand options.

Tangible. Get ideas out of your head. Sketches and prototypes let us see, hear, taste, smell, touch, share, and change what we think. When we render our mental models to distributed cognition and iterative design, we realise an intelligence greater than ourselves.

Agile. Plan to improvise. Clarify the extent to which the goal, path, and process are fixed or flexible. Be aware of feedback and options. Know both the plan and change must happen. Embrace adventure.

Reflective. Question paths, goals, and beliefs. Start and finish with a beginner's mind. Try experiments to test hypotheses and metrics to spot errors. Use experience and metacognition to grow wisdom.

Second, we can get better at planning by practicing the skills of framing, imagining, narrowing, deciding, executing, and reflecting. It may help to think of them as phases, but as planning is nonlinear, each practice may occur at any stage.

Framing. While common sense suggests we should start to plan by defining goals, it also helps to study the lens through which we see problems and solutions. By examining needs, wants, feelings, and beliefs, we're better able to know and share our vision and values.

Imagining. By expanding our awareness of paths and possibilities, we create choice and inform strategy. We search and research for information, then play with models to stray beyond knowledge. Sketches draw insights that help us add options and refine plans.

Narrowing. After diverging, it's critical to converge by prioritizing paths and options. This requires study of drivers, levers, estimates, and consequences, as the value of a strategy is tied to time and risk.

Deciding. While decisions are often made in an instant, the process of committing to and communicating a course of action merits time and attention. Instructions are essential to the rendering of intent. Words matter. So do numbers. Define metrics for success carefully.

Executing. The dichotomy between planning and doing is false. In all sorts of contexts, we plan as we travel, build, or get things done.

Reflecting. While it helps to ask questions throughout the process, we should also make space to look back at the whole from the end.

Long before the invention of time, people used the North Star to find their way in the dark. In the future, I hope you will use these principles and practices to make your way in the world.

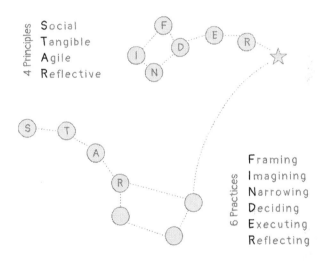

Figure 1-10. Principles and practices of planning.

Myths of Tomorrow

Not long after booking our tour of the Actun Tunichil Muknal cave in Belize, I woke up in the middle of the night in a cold sweat. To assess our risks, I'd been reading about mosquitos, botflies, scorpions, spiders, and snakes, and unfortunately a fer-de-lance had slithered into my nightmares. The next day I dug into statistics and convinced myself we'd be safe. And we were. The natural beauty and ancient artifacts of the cave are magical, and we escaped the underworld unscathed. In our week in Belize, we never even saw a snake, but we did enjoy surprises. In the sea, we swam with sharks, turtles and rays, and in the jungle we met a newborn donkey named Valentina. Also, in traveling dirt roads, we saw barefoot children, dogs, chickens, goats and ramshackle cottages, and Claudia said "I wish we grew up here." That was a surprise. So we asked her to explain. It was the children at play in the dirt. They looked happy and carefree. We don't see that so much where we live.

I tell this story as a reminder, for myself as much as for you, that we can't have adventure without risk. I aim to inspire us to go towards the fear. Isn't that the point of the tales we tell, to change belief and behavior? Myths are stories of the past designed to shape the future. The ritual sacrifice of children in a dark cave was a desperate attempt by the Maya to appease the rain God and calm their people in times of drought.

This book opens with the words of Malala Yousafzai, "One child, one teacher, one book, one pen can change the world."[46] Malala is named after Afghanistan's folk hero, Malalai of Maiwand. In a legendary battle in 1880 against the British, the Afghans had lost hope and begun to retreat, when a teenage girl lifted her veil as a flag and raised her voice to roar "it is better to live like a lion for one day than to live like a slave for a hundred years."[47] She led the army to victory but was shot and died on the battlefield. Today, much like her namesake, Malala lives a life that myths are made of. As a teenager in Pakistan, she stood up for the education of girls and was nearly murdered by the Taliban. Nevertheless, she persisted.

Malala is an advocate for girls' education and women's equality, a student at Oxford University, and the youngest ever Nobel Prize laureate. She is also a story we tell ourselves to shape a better future. Malala reminds us "we realize the importance of our voices only when we are silenced."[48] When the Taliban burned schools and banned girls, she used her blog to roar like a lion. As a preteen Muslim girl, she dared to challenge the patriarchy, and her voice was heard around the world. Malala and her family could never have predicted or planned for what happened next. She nearly died at the hands of the Taliban and her family fled to the United Kingdom, but Malala never lost spirit. Instead, she used her platform as the world's most famous teenager to create the Malala Fund, a nonprofit dedicated to "working for a world where every girl can learn and lead without fear." She has upheld her values even as her context, role, and goals have shifted dramatically. Her story helps us to realise our own power to change.

In this chapter you may have noticed and perhaps even been irritated by the inconsistent spelling of realise and realize. It's not a mistake but a subtle gesture to surface a delicate point. Different isn't wrong. I am British and American, and this book will be read in many countries, so neither spelling is right or wrong. When in doubt, we're told to pick one and be consistent. But why? Is it to maintain the illusion there's one right way? Is it because diversity is inefficient? I invite you to ask if some irregularities that irritate may also inform. Why do they cause anger? What do you fear? What might they teach?

Our thoughts and feelings about difference matter more than we know. To embrace different cultures is to learn new ways, to be open to growth is to experiment, and to nurture options is to engage in meta strategy. When Ralph Waldo Emerson wrote "a foolish consistency is the hobgoblin of little minds,"[49] he was inviting us to be free. That's what I'm doing too. We are traveling through the best and worst of times, and even in the dark, it's not hard to see we need new stories and rituals.

Planning matters more than we realize because that word not only has two spellings, but multiple meanings too. We might realize things are going downhill and get out early, or we may see a way to turn things around, and realise a better outcome. That's the promise of the design of paths and goals and the aim of our mnemonic star finder. It takes vision and spirit, and there's no one right way, but if we dare, we can make real the futures we want by bearing myths and *what ifs* into the world.

Framing

"I will show you fear in a handful of dust."
– T. S. ELIOT

At 14,259 feet, Longs Peak is the highest summit in Colorado's Rocky Mountain National Park. In summer, day hikers can reach the top without climbing gear. The 15 mile trek takes 10 to 15 hours. The views are breathtaking. In 2016, lured by its siren song, I arrived at the trailhead of the Keyhole route with backpack and headlamp at 4 a.m. The night sky was beautiful. A few hours later, I made it over a boulder field to the keyhole which serves as a gateway to narrow ledges and steep inclines. The wind was fierce. I began to have doubts, resolved to forge ahead, but on the threshold, I froze in fear. After a moment of abject terror, I crept to safety and began my untimely descent.

It didn't take long to conclude I was happy with the outcome. I'm a hiker not a climber. The decision to try was made lightly. It's my habit to value grit, but in planning this book and this trip, I'd chosen to experiment with commitment. So why risk my life for an unforced goal? Also, the summit was actually a subgoal. Each year I choose a quest, be it a mountain or a marathon, that inspires me to exercise and eat well. I'd already put in the work. As I wandered my way down, I felt happy and carefree. But later that day as I told my wife, she surprised me by asking "so when will you try again?" She didn't get it. I had nothing to prove. I was happy to let it go. Or so I thought.

Figure 2-1. Framing is how we understand and explain our plans.

It's easy to say the first step in planning is to define your goals, but it's also simplistic. In deciding to climb a mountain, there's more than meets the eye. What's the trigger that makes us take aim? What beliefs or feelings can get us to pivot? What's the vision or value that helps us endure? Framing is the practice through which we understand and explain the why, what, and how. It starts as we begin to plan but may not stop when we're done. I'm reframing my Longs Peak odyssey now, as I write.

To do this work, we employ metaphors and mental models as shortcuts. A ferocious battle to the summit activates the frame of war, whereas talk of solitude in the wild invokes the insight and wisdom of a spiritual quest. Frames are heuristics or rules of thumb we use to make sense of information. A category is a frame, and so is a stereotype. We're mostly not aware of these maps even as we make plans built on their keys and contours.

Understanding the Problem

Nobody relies on improvisation more than the Marine Corps, which explains why the Marines respect planning. They must be prepared to rapidly deploy a combined arms task force to deal with a crisis anywhere in the world; and units in the field must execute the mission while adapting the plan as needed.

The *Marine Corps Planning Process* includes six steps: problem framing, course of action development, wargaming, course of action comparison and decision, orders development, and transition to execution; and it defines the first step as pivotal.

> Problem framing enhances understanding of the environment and the nature of the problem. It identifies what the command must accomplish, when and where it must be done and, most importantly, why – the purpose. Since no amount of subsequent planning can solve a problem insufficiently understood, problem framing is the most important step in planning. [1]

I agree with the Marines in spirit, but I have a problem with their framing. A focus on "understanding the problem" can become part of the problem. In our model, framing includes understanding and explaining both the problem and solution.

If you see this argument as semantic, you're right. Words are levers. A small change can have a big impact. In framing, it's helpful to recognize that how, and whether, we see a problem is invisibly shaped by our awareness of potential solutions.

As an information architect, framing is a vital part of my work, but it's not what organizations ask me to do. For example, the National Cancer Institute hired me to fix the usability of their website by reorganizing its navigation. The goal was to reduce the number of clicks from the home page to content. But I soon discovered a bigger problem. Most folks searching for answers about specific types of cancer never reached cancer.gov due to poor findability via Google. I only saw this problem because I knew how to solve it. I explained to my client that by aligning the information architecture with search engine optimization, we could improve usability and findability. Together, we were able to reframe the goals. The site went on to win awards and rise to the top of the American Customer Satisfaction Index.

We all chuckle at the old adage "To a man with a hammer, everything looks like a nail," but we each fail to realize how our own idiosyncratic toolbox shapes what we see. To address this blind spot, we must be explicit about the messy, nonlinear paths binding understand the problem to explain the solution.

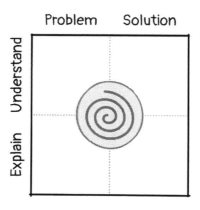

Figure 2-2. Framing is messy and nonlinear.

Also, we may see anew with a semantic twist. I didn't climb Longs Peak to solve a problem. I did it for fun. What if we aim framing at *realising an opportunity* that lives in the fertile space between what is and what might be? This frame opens a door to innovation and the solving of problems that don't exist.

A word for our problem is fixity. We're fixed on our maps and fail to see the territory. This is why 911 calls from people lost in corn mazes is a thing. It doesn't occur to them to push aside the stalks, since they think they're in a maze, not a cornfield.

The nine dot puzzle shows how mental models can be traps.

> Given a sheet of paper with nine dots in a square matrix, each
> equidistant from its neighbors, join all the dots with no more than
> four continuous straight lines. Don't lift the pencil from the paper.

If you've never wrangled with this problem, try it now. It can
seem impossible until you've seen the solution. Less than ten
percent of people are able to solve the nine dot problem within
ten minutes, despite the fact it can be solved by using one,
two, three, or four continuous straight lines or paths. I won't
reveal the answers here, they're easily findable online, but the
trick lies in freeing ourselves from self-imposed constraints.

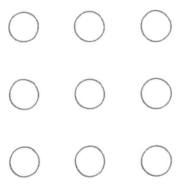

Figure 2-3. The nine dot problem.

To evade fixity, it helps to embrace multimethod research. On
consulting projects, I mix stakeholder meetings, user research
and ethnography, surveys, analytics, and participatory design.
I listen as my clients define scope and explain the problem, but
nurture my inner contrarian and work to keep an open mind.

It's overwhelming to absorb myriad sources of qualitative and
quantitative data, but it enables me to wonder outside the box.
What's the problem? What's the root cause? And what is it we
hope to improve? Is it software, a website, a system, a service,

a place, or an experience? Each frame opens a new window of opportunity. Discovery plus reflection leads to better goals.

I wasn't always so mindful. As an entrepreneur in the 1990s, I had a growth mindset. I defined "Big Hairy Audacious Goals" and worked hard to achieve them.[2] Most years, our consulting firm more than doubled in income and staff, and it felt good. To create jobs, help clients, make the web better for users, and profit all at the same time was great for my ego. It was easy to be addicted to growth and to see *get bigger faster* as the goal. I don't have many regrets from those days, but I am grateful for the downturn that forced us to close. I'm happier and healthier now, because I realised the opportunity to slow down then.

Our culture is defined by growth. We rate countries by gross domestic product and companies by market capitalization. We label people by grade, title, and income. We define goals and measure progress to achieve success. We're inspired by Walt Disney who said "a person should set his goals as early as he can and devote all his energy to getting there"[3] and "all our dreams can come true, if we have the courage to pursue them."[4] In Disney's relentless quest to "make people happy," he built a global empire that's worth more than $150 billion.

In our pursuit of happiness, we heed the timeless words of management guru Peter Drucker who told us "if you can't measure it, you can't manage it." We define key performance indicators (KPIs) and objectives and key results (OKRs) for business. And we use wearable sensors to track steps, calories, insulin levels, and the heart rates of individuals. The numbers keep us so busy, we fail to realize Drucker would never have said those words. The quote is also attributed to W. Edwards Deming, but what he really said is "it is wrong to suppose that if you can't measure it, you can't manage it – a costly myth."[5]

Do you ever wonder why misquotations are so common? Is it sloth or greed? I suspect all seven deadly sins. To make a case for a goal, we're seduced by the fit of words and symbols. I'd love to tell you "not everything that counts can be counted, and not everything that can be counted counts" is the wise counsel of Albert Einstein, but it's not. The prevalence of misquotations affords a glimpse into the harmful side effects of goal setting. As the authors of *Goals Gone Wild* argue, the damages are far more serious and systematic than we realize.

> The beneficial effects of goal setting have been overstated and the systematic harm caused by goal setting has been largely ignored. Side effects include a narrow focus that neglects non-goal areas, a rise in unethical behavior, distorted risk preferences, corrosion of organizational culture, and reduced intrinsic motivation.[6]

You know who had goals? Enron. Of course, I don't mean to say goals and metrics are bad. They are vital to inspiration and motivation. But they are dangerous. It's all too easy to fix on a target and miss the point. That's why we must reflect on our needs, wants, feelings, values, and beliefs, as well as our goals.

The problem is reflection is harder than it sounds. I felt this in planning to climb Longs Peak the second time. Months after my initial attempt, the mountain was on my mind, when I got a surprise invitation to speak in Boulder in early September. It felt like fate. I decided to try again. But this time I would plan my way to the top. I bought a helmet and gloves, devised an intense physical training program, and started my research.

I didn't get far. This mountain is scary. Before my first try, I ignored trip reports to evade anxiety. Now I made myself dig in, so I'd know what to expect. Past the keyhole are narrow ledges with 2,000 foot drops, steep inclines with loose rock, and a slick granite slab that requires near vertical scrambling. The weather is unpredictable, so you can't ever count out ice or lightning. The wind is insane with gusts up to 200 mph. If conditions change unexpectedly, climbers may make mortal decisions influenced by fatigue and altitude sickness. Deaths, injuries, and helicopter rescues are a regular occurrence. Of course, most folks survive intact, with only two deaths for every 10,000 summits, but I found little solace in this statistic.

I chose to focus on training and not think about the climb, but soon ran into a problem. My foot hurt, a lot. At first I thought it was metatarsalgia, but the way it would come and go made no sense. I realized it was pain rooted in repressed emotion, a mind-body connection I'd endured before.[7] This was about the mountain. The emotion at the root of the problem was fear.

I thought about quitting but read *The Art of Fear* instead. The author, Kristen Ulmer, rose to fame as an extreme skier, then reinvented herself as a *mindset coach* to help rid folks of pain, anxiety, anger, and depression caused by avoidance of fear. Noting even a single-cell amoeba, exposed to fire, moves away to save itself, she explains fear is a signal from the oldest, most deeply buried part of our brain, and that whether we call it an amygdala or a lizard brain, we must listen when it talks, since repressed fear is a key source of injury, illness, addiction, and rage. Of course, System 1 doesn't use words, so we often don't know what it means. Even so, as Kristen notes, we respond in powerful ways, such as the translation of fear into fierceness.

> Ask pro athletes – preferably after their careers are over and they have no more illusions about themselves or their hype – what made them great. They'll eventually admit that it was the perfect storm of many things, but mostly the right childhood demons and fears. Perhaps a need to prove something to someone. Or fear of, as with me, not being special, of being invisible, of not being loved, or of failure and rejection. This is what makes for a great athlete.[8]

We can't conquer fear, but we can use it. Even better, we can render the emotion into a source of joy and wisdom. To begin, we must become curious about the roles of fear in our lives.

Fear is the motive. That's what I realised in my goal to reach the summit. Fear of disease and death moves me to exercise. The thrill of fear inspires me to climb. I don't need to scale the mountain. But I want to. Risk is a way to feel alive. Fear is also a barrier, quite often invisible. Most goals are never more than a fleeting glimpse. We undo them with the first twinge of fear. If I'd known then what I know now, I'd have erased the idea of Longs Peak before it became a goal. But the journey altered my framing of the destination. To study and relish my fear of heights became an explicit co-goal. My curiosity was piqued. My foot no longer hurt. I began to run towards the fear.

Explaining the Solution

A plan is a frame. If asked to make a plan, you may see steps on a path to a goal, but that's not the only way. A plan can be a process. Innovation sends us off the map in search of fuzzy goals. Before we define a solution, it's worth exploring which elements might be fixed or flexible. In a waterfall model, the scope is fixed while time and cost are flexible. We define the goal precisely, then struggle to stay on schedule and budget. In agile frameworks, time and cost are fixed while scope is flexible. Goals may change based on progress and feedback.

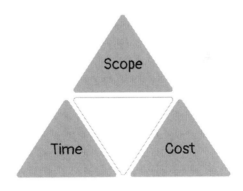

Figure 2-4. The iron triangle of planning.

The iron triangle tells us "good, fast, cheap: pick two," but like all maps, it hides more than it reveals. A better way may exist, if we think outside the triangle. A new tool or technology can do the trick, or we might invest in infrastructure. This needn't be complex. A simple kitchen reorg can lead to faster, cheaper, better meals. The solution exists in the flexibility of our minds.

As we shift from understanding the problem to explaining the solution, we should mind our frames. The way we perceive an opportunity may not be the best way to sell it, but here lie dragons. Aristotle defined rhetoric as "observing in any given case the available means of persuasion,"[9] and as George Lakoff warns, framing is among the most powerful of those means.

> Frames are mental structures that shape the way we see the world. As a result, they shape the goals we seek, the plans we make, the way we act, and what counts as a good or bad outcome.[10]

Frames are evoked by words, and as a colleague of mine likes to say "words make people hallucinate."[11] In a debate, Lakoff argues their language draws you into their worldview, so do not use their words, like Richard Nixon did when he claimed "I am not a crook."[12] Of course, framing isn't the only path to persuasion. In *Influence*, Robert Cialdini shares a panoply of tricks. For instance, in the case of a person who wants to skip to the front of a line, the subtle shift from "May I use the Xerox machine?" to "May I use the Xerox machine, because I have to make some copies?" boosts compliance from 60 to 93 percent. People respond to an explicitly stated reason, even if it adds no information. The word "because" exploits a cognitive bias to elicit automatic compliance.[13] Similarly, price is a trigger for quality. Salespeople take advantage of the mental shortcut or stereotype that "expensive equals good" all the time. Age, sex, race, and religion are also triggers. As I said, here lie dragons.

Cialdini's cons are intriguing but easily blur from persuasion into manipulation. Our frames must be guided by our values. Of course, it's possible to frameshift ethically. For instance, if you're motivated to start a company by fears of climate change and ecosystem collapse, and hope to attract investors across the political spectrum, it may make sense to frame the solution in terms of clean or local energy. It's not wrong to reframe an argument in a way that resonates with your audience, but it is unethical to trick people into acting against their own interests or acting on misinformation. Frames exist on a slippery slope.

That's why we must take time to wallow in the problem space and in the solution space before fixing on a frame. In the back and forth between what is and what might be, we may realise the kind of opportunity where the solution sells itself. In 1997, the folks who built and sold computers were fixed on features and performance, yet upon returning to save Apple, Steve Jobs argued "You've got to start with the customer experience and work backwards to the technology."[14] This reframing of the experience as the product opened a path to the reinvention of computers. The insight arose in a mind willing to wallow in the uncomfortable spaces that bridge problem and solution.

Principles to Practices

Before we turn the page from framing to imagining, let's recall our mnemonic by asking a question: how might we make the practice of framing more social, tangible, agile, and reflective?

We can make framing social by creatively engaging people in the definition of goals and vision. We might employ the usual methods in unusual ways, or try uncommon methods. Before building the Eishin school and campus in Japan, the architect Christopher Alexander inspired teachers and students to share their needs, wants, and desires with this gentle invitation.

> Please close your eyes. Just keep your eyes closed and dream. Imagine a place, the most wonderful school you can imagine, a kind of fairytale school where everyone is happy.[15]

Reluctantly, hesitatingly, they would begin to describe their hopes and feelings in word-pictures the architect later used to create a pattern language for the community. Visions include "the library has a large, quiet reading room on the second floor, with shelves and tables and carrels and beautiful windows," and "there is also one garden, so secret, that it does not appear on any map." It's a lovely and unusual illustration of participatory design, and it worked. I visited the school a quarter century after it was built. The whole campus is full of life and beauty. No place has ever made me feel more happy.

Do you have a fleeting glimpse that may become a goal? How can you make framing more social? There are more ways than stars in the universe. Most require that we also make framing more tangible. For instance, Jeff Bezos has created a culture at Amazon in which "working backwards" is an assumption. For any new initiative, employees begin by writing a press release and FAQ that explain the finished product to the customer. [16] No product is built without conversations and iterations around these tangible artifacts of a customer-centered frame.

Of course, we can also make "working forwards" social and tangible as well. Designers use all sorts of methods to make the invisible visible, so we can talk about needs and wants. A mood board is a collage of images, text, and color that invites us to chat about feel, flow, and style. A mental model diagram shows how people think, feel, and act by organizing tasks into boxes into towers. A set of core desired feelings exposes flaws in material goals. And a mind map can uncover relationships between co-goals, values, and beliefs, so we can get feedback.

One way to be agile from the start is to stop building products and focus on "jobs to be done." [17] Why does a customer *hire* a kettle? Is it to boil water? Or to brew a beverage? Keurig gets the whole job done on a single platform. Outcome-driven innovation starts with framing for agility. We might also step back to frame the goal in terms of intent, as why expands how. If the goal is to get in shape, do you need to run a marathon?

The last point of our star is reflective, and it's what framing is all about. Our choice of words and metaphors says as much about us as the goal. Is it a game or a conversation or a battle, and why do we frame it that way? My friend is a life coach, and she says eighty percent of her clients are not ready to plan, because they don't trust or listen to themselves. How can you know what you want if you don't even know who you are?

We're not always free to choose our goals. In school, it's hard to escape grades. At work, metrics roll top down. It's safest to go with the flow and accept the goals defined by the system. Even so it pays to reflect. If we study the maps that make the system, it's easier to win the game. And if we identify co-goals or frame the goals we're given as part of our mission, we can inspire ourselves. And we may be more free than we think. Much of what we do is due to want not need. Food, water, clothing, shelter, and fellowship are essential, yet we mostly sacrifice to gain status and to stave off the emotion of fear.

My second ascent of Longs Peak began as the first, under a clear night sky with infinite stars. The goal was also clear: to explore my fears on the ledges and slopes beyond the keyhole. I had a great plan, an early start, and hiked up the forest path in high spirits, but as the sun and I rose above the tree line, the wind began to roar. There were others on the mountain, and some turned back. Resolute, I carried on. The wind got worse. The gusts were like nothing I'd ever felt. I had to kneel to not be blown over and shut my eyes to stop the dust. Reluctantly, I realized I'd never make it past the keyhole. So I turned back, again. On the way down, I heard one climber reached the top, most quit, and one was blown over, a face of grit and blood.

I'm not sure I was made to climb mountains, or at least not mountains so tall. It's not the hard work. I love that. But my tolerance for risk is low. On the other hand, I'm glad I made the summit my goal. I learned to be curious about fear. To plan backwards makes sense. A clear goal helps us endure.

But grit can blind us to insight. Pema Chödrön says "fear is a natural reaction to moving closer to the truth."[18] I agree. Now, in framing my goals, I'm more likely to go towards the fear.

Imagining

"When I invent things,
I do not use language."

– TEMPLE GRANDIN

Before our oldest daughter Claire began driver education, I took her to an empty parking lot. She didn't want her first time behind the wheel to be with a stranger. We covered the basics, drove a few laps, and practiced parking. Once she'd built confidence, in the midst of a lap, I yelled "stop!" Claire hit the accelerator, realized her mistake, and hit the brake. I smiled. She was furious. But the next time, she got it right.

Two years later, her sister turned fifteen. I had the same plan. After a few laps, I asked Claudia to park. She carefully crept into the space, hit the gas, ran the curb, drove up a grass hill, caught her error, and hit the brake. I was too stunned to yell "stop." After taking a moment, I stated "that was not good." We reversed down the hill and continued the lesson. I aimed for minimal trauma, and it worked. Claudia felt confident by the time we went home. The only lasting damage was a dent.

But I was upset with myself. I realized I should have had both girls practice the move from accelerator to brake while the car was still in park. If I'd spent a few minutes imagining different ways to teach this skill, I could have reduced the risk. But isn't that often the case? We take the obvious path to a goal. Only if something goes wrong do we play the counterfactual game of *what if*. And this usually makes sense. Automatic pilot is good enough for the multitude of minor goals we juggle every day.

Figure 3-1. Imagining expands paths and possibilities.

But some goals merit attention. When big risks or rewards are at stake, we must make time to question our maps and mental models, search for new options, and play with prototypes. In the hopeful practice of imagining, there's always a better way.

Willpower and Waypower

In *The Psychology of Hope*, Charles Snyder recalls his childhood in Iowa and what he learned by fishing with Grandpa Gus.

> He would ask me what kind of fish we were going after – northern pike, walleye, bass, crappie, or catfish. Now, you might ask, what difference can that make? Well, a lot. If you want to catch a bass, you go about it differently than if you are after some other kind of

fish. Grandpa Gus was teaching me the importance of being clear about my goal. Once we had decided what we were fishing for, Gus seemed to become even more certain we would succeed. He would tell me to think about how great it would be to catch a fat bass. In his mind's eye, he could see it happening. I could, too.[1]

Charles explains that even on the rare occasions when they weren't catching anything, Gus was always experimenting.

Opening his battered aluminum tackle box, he looked over trays that revealed every lure and bait imaginable. And he would use most of them. The menu of live baits included such delicacies as worms, leeches, grasshoppers, and minnows. We would fish in shallow water, in deep water, beside weed beds, near docks, in open water, on and on. We might anchor and still fish, cast, drift, or troll. He would teach me to move my rod tip in different ways. Sometimes we would fish in the morning, sometimes at night. Gus was an experimenter willing to try new things. He said that much of the fun and excitement came from changing how we fished.[2]

Gus taught his grandson more than how to fish. Charles went on to pioneer the field of positive psychology and to invent the science of hope. The formula at the heart of his lifework states that hope equals willpower plus waypower. So where there's a will, you may not find a way, without the full sum of hope.

Waypower reflects the mental plans or road maps that guide hopeful thought. Waypower is a mental capacity we can call on to find one or more effective ways to reach our goals.[3]

His research, which includes administering the "hope scale" to more than 10,000 people, shows hope is not an emotion but a mindset rooted in the belief that you will find a way. And we don't all have an equal share. Folks with "big will, little ways" respond to brick walls by pushing harder, whereas those with "little will, big ways" are haunted by unrealised ideas and plans. In contrast, high hopers know they have the creativity and discipline to achieve big goals. Not blind optimists, they are problem solvers who invent a way around every obstacle.

Defining the optimal route to every goal is neither practical nor possible, but we can build waypower and find better paths to priority goals through the practice of imagining. As we shift from why to how, we must expand our awareness of potential ways to connect the dots. Imagine a night sky so clear the stars blur into a milky way. Countless stars go unseen and there are infinitely more constellations. This truth holds for steps, paths, and plans. The road more traveled is obvious but often it's not the best. Necessity gives birth to invention but why wait? The mother of imagination is sassy and knows there's a better way.

Search for Options

To start, we must revisit framing. A clear goal lifts willpower but perhaps at the expense of waypower. To manage this tradeoff in the military, plans that specify targets must also describe intent. Similarly, in the business of innovation, we employ fuzzy goals to nurture creativity. Framing is a path-limiting step, so we must take time to search for fitting goals.

When I was a child, I saw a raven attack a blackbird with a broken wing. I ran to the small bird and lifted it gently with cupped hands. The raven began to caw and swoop and smite the back of my head. I was terrified but determined to protect the blackbird. My dad heard the ruckus, ran outside, and told me to let go of the baby crow, so its mom would let me be. In teaching her child to fly, she taught me that it's harder to help than we may think, and it's risky to act before understanding.

I tell this story to introduce the relationship between planning and search. In the moment, the only source I could search was my mind. My plan to save a bird was a product of the memory and imagination of a seven year old. I had no time to seek answers in a library or book. Google didn't exist. And I saw no way to query reality by running an experiment. So I ran with a plan based on an error, and it didn't go well. Sometimes that's the best we can do. But not always. For important goals when time allows, we can use information, experience and our rich imaginations to test and refine the beliefs that form our paths.

Let's say you plan to teach a class on a subject you know well. How do you begin? You might create a syllabus, then prepare lectures for each topic in the outline. But is there a better way? Remember, you enjoy access to information and aren't limited to trial and error. Perhaps you find a book called *Make It Stick* about the science of successful learning and encounter another mnemonic, RIGOR, that helps you teach different and better. [4]

Retrieval. Learning is deeper and more durable when effortful, so add desirable difficulties. We rapidly lose 70% of what we read or hear, and rereading or repeating – massed practice – is ineffective. Tests before and after lessons that require retrieval from memory or "forced recall" improve retention by more than 50%.

Interleaving. To organize lectures into discrete topics is obvious and ineffective. While it's harder and slower to mix topics, skills, and problem types, interleaving can improve performance by 215% by forcing us to recall, compare, contrast, and understand context.

Garnishing. Memory is like Velcro. [5] To connect new ideas to what we already know adds hooks and loops. Invite students to garnish new knowledge by explaining it in their own words and contexts.

Organization. Ask students to extract key ideas into mind maps, and play with alternative ways of organizing these mental models, to improve their ability to recall and transfer ideas across contexts.

Reflection. To reflect look back and within. People who extract principles from experiences learn better. Ask students to think about how they learn. Metacognition is an invisible superpower.

Would this new information change your plan? Are lectures by a sage on the stage the best way to teach? Or might you flip the classroom with instruction online and homework in class? That would allow students to ask you and their peers for help.

But as a little bird taught me, it's harder to help than we think. Edgar Schein, the guru of organizational culture, wrote an odd little book on *Helping* that opens with a story about directions.

> Outside my house, a woman in her car drove up and asked me "How do I get to Massachusetts Avenue?" I asked her where she was headed and learned that she wanted to go to downtown Boston. I then pointed out that the road she was on led directly to downtown, and she did not need Mass Ave. She thanked me profusely for not sending her to the street she had asked for.[6]

Schein explains that the path to "helpful help" begins with "humble inquiry," which reminds me of lessons I learned in library school on how to conduct a reference interview. We progress from open questions like "how may I help you?" to sensemaking by asking "how will you use the information?" If we hope to help people with goals, we must search for intent.

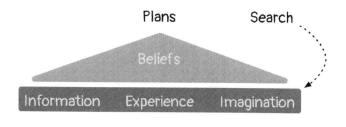

Figure 3-2. Search may shift beliefs and plans.

Might humble inquiry change how you plan to teach? Are you clear on what students know and need? In design, we realize "you are not the user" and rely on ethnography, interviews, usability tests, and analytics to research beliefs and behaviors. Adapt these tools to your goals. Empathy will shift your plans.

I also learned in library school how to search for information and how to evaluate sources for truth and bias. In the swirl of social media, fake news, and alternative facts, these core skills of information literacy have never been more essential. If you search for confirmation, you will find it, but dare the opposite and self-correction may bear truth and more successful plans.

Of course, information has limits, so we must also search the world as it is via play and practice. In *Making Learning Whole*, David Perkins argues education should be more playful. To teach for understanding, we must make games worth playing.

> Our real criterion of understanding has to be performance. People understand something when they can think and act flexibly with what they know about it, not just recall information and execute routine skills.[7]

Physical, intellectual, and emotional engagement is vital for cultivating motivation, imagination, and openness to change.

> Mental models are the game board of the mind. Learning often means changing the game board, not just learning fancier strategies on the same board with the same pieces. Often the game board we begin with incorporates mistakes and blind spots and prejudices.[8]

David Perkins writes "our most important choice is what we try to teach."[9] I agree. But equally vital is his insight that when we teach the wrong way, there's no will. To use simulations and experiments to search inspires both students and teachers.

Similarly, architects use models to imagine space into place. As Christopher Alexander teamed with teachers and students to render word-pictures into a pattern language for the Eishin campus, he also began to search the land for inspiration.

> He and his team mapped the topography – land forms, slopes, trees, ridges, roads – of the physical site. They then began the hard work of bringing the two systems of centers, patterns and places, together into a simple, beautiful site plan. They planted hundreds of six foot tall bamboo sticks topped with colorful ribbons to identify places, spaces, and relationships. By seeing-moving these flags for months, they were able to *discover* the plan. They augmented this visualization with topographic models of the site, using pieces of balsa wood for buildings. After trial and error, they fit these patterns and places into a wonderful, generative whole.[10]

In design, we use sketches to explore paths for software and websites. While folks often rush to build high fidelity working prototypes, simple models are best for imagining. In the 1990s, Jeff Hawkins cut a block of wood to fit his shirt pocket, and carried it around for months, pretending it was a computer. He used a chopstick as a stylus and tested interfaces sketched on paper and glued to the block. People thought he was crazy.

> I walked around answering calls with this block of wood, and of course it didn't do anything. I did it to see if it worked. I decided it worked pretty well.[11]

This odd experiment launched the PalmPilot, the world's first successful handheld computer, a decade before the iPhone. All too often we rush to build fancy prototypes, so we can impress executives and gain support. Most paths are eliminated early without due diligence, and we don't even know what we miss. Simple models are best for play. Low fidelity lets us delay commitment to one path. Rough sketches keep options open.

Figure 3-3. Reframe the goal as intent.

To be free is to have options, and the first step to freedom is awareness. To overcome option blindness, we must reframe the goal as intent. This embiggens the goal, making it easier to score from many angles. If today's goal is to have my daughter drive laps around a parking lot, it won't occur to me to ask her to practice the switch from accelerator to brake while the car's in park in our driveway. But if my intent is to help her build competence and confidence as a driver, the options multiply, and I can imagine all sorts of paths towards this larger goal.

To raise awareness of options, we must engage in divergent and emergent thinking. We open minds to a broad spectrum of possibility by being playful. To get ideas to flow, we defer all criticism. Otherwise, we may dismiss viable paths due to false belief, cognitive bias, and fear. We suspend disbelief to set free our imagination. We embrace the belief there's always a better way, because waypower is a sassy mindset. We grow as many possible paths as possible. The time to prune is later.

In *The Black Swan*, Nassim Nicholas Taleb eviscerates the idea that we can predict the future.

> The computer, the Internet, and the laser; all three were unplanned, unpredicted, and unappreciated upon their discovery, and remained unappreciated well after their initial use. They were consequential. They were black swans.[12]

A black swan is an improbable or inconceivable event with massive impact.[13] To feel safe and smart, we rewrite history and memory to suggest we saw it coming. Google was a black swan, as was 9/11. Since we can't predict, Taleb tells us to follow the example of the ancient Greek philosopher Thales.

> He put a down payment on the seasonal use of every olive press in the vicinity of Miletus and Chios, which he got at low rent. The harvest turned out to be extremely bountiful and there was demand for olive presses, so he released the owners of olive presses on his own terms, building a fortune in the process.[14]

In finance, this is known as the first-ever options trade in recorded history. Nobody knew if the harvest would be good or bad. Thales used a deposit to buy the right but not the obligation, enabling him to benefit from the positive side of uncertainty without facing an equal risk on the negative side.

There are countless mundane opportunities to create options. When our girls played travel sports, I learned to book hotels before we knew the schedule. I'd guess the tournaments we'd play, book rooms, and when wrong I'd cancel online for free. If I waited for the schedule, the best hotels would be sold out.

Figure 3-4. Options let you be stupid.

The story of the olive presses isn't about being so smart you see the future. Rather, the moral is options let you be stupid. In an uncertain world, the path of least steps may not be the best. When two roads diverge, an option lets you travel both.

Principles to Practices

How might we make imagining more social, tangible, agile, and reflective? To address the first point in our guiding star, we can ask for help. Invite a diverse mix of folks to a planning workshop. Ask them to reframe the goal as intent, brainstorm divergent paths, and imagine unorthodox options. Or, engage a partner in the project. People are likely to generate more helpful help when they share goals and have skin in the game.

Philanthropy is a noble goal that often fails its intent. In Africa, donated mosquito nets are used to fish, so ecosystems crash as malaria soars; and food aid undercuts local farmers, adding to the problem of hunger. In the 1990s, people imagined a better way by applying "positive deviance" to the stubborn problem of malnutrition in Vietnam. [15] Researchers asked villagers to identify unusually healthy children. Via ethnography, they found their families gathered foods considered unsuitable for children (*shrimp, crab, sweet potato greens*). Also, contrary to cultural norms, these deviants fed their kids four times a day and washed their hands before and after meals. A nutrition program based on these insights was created, and it worked. In two years, malnutrition fell by 85 percent. It's hard to help but not impossible, if you use co-creation to find a better way.

We can make imagining more social and tangible by playing the games of *Gamestorming*.[16] Mission Impossible opens minds by taking an existing design, shifting a core aspect to make it "impossible," and inviting folks to help solve the problem.

How do we build a house...in a day?

How do we create a mobile device...with no battery?

In Affinity Map, we might ask "how can we reach our vision," then collect and organize ideas on sticky notes or index cards. Pre-Mortem gets folks gamestorming what could possibly go wrong. And Post the Path gets people to sketch the steps in a process, first as individuals, then working together as a group.

There's always a way to play. In planning a backpacking trip several years ago, I read and made lists, but I also tried things out. In our yard, I burned my finger on the pocket stove, then learned how to foil the wind. In the living room, I modeled an "emergency poncho" for my wife. She laughed until she cried. Thinner than a dry-cleaning bag, it would have been ripped to shreds by foliage. She found me a real poncho. In our bathtub, I tested the water filter, since learning by failure feels like a game until someone gets larval cysts in their brain. We learn too late when we fail to fit practice and play into planning.[17]

The Marines are experts in the shift from tangible to agile. Options for how the goal and intent might be accomplished are illustrated through course of action development.

The graphic and narrative portray how the organization will accomplish the mission. Together the graphic and narrative identify who, when, what, where, how, and why (intent).[18]

Paths are then tested by wargaming at varying levels of fidelity from *what if* conversations to computer simulations to military exercises. The purpose of wargaming is to select and improve the right plan. In design, we may use bodystorming. By engaging the mind, body, and environment in play, we're apt to develop more agile people, organizations, and plans.

In *Bright Lights, No City* Whit Alexander, inventor of Cranium, sets out to help people by starting a for-profit business selling rechargeable batteries to off-grid villagers in Ghana. His belief in social entrepreneurship is inspired by a dichotomy, coined by William Easterly, that divides helpers into two categories.

> Planners have created a culture of freebies in the third world that makes it difficult for market forces to find a viable niche. When a charity gives away mosquito nets, what happens to the local entrepreneur who is trying to make and sell mosquito nets for a reasonable profit, running a business that employs villagers and sustains itself? The Searchers are experimenters who don't claim to have all the answers but are willing to hit the ground and find out, especially if it leads to some personal reward. Searchers have better incentives and better results.[19]

I'm no fan of this dichotomy. Plan and search belong together. But I do see entrepreneurs as agile in ways philanthropists are not. Whit's company, Burro, now sells solar lights and mobile phone chargers. Relentlessly, the market will find a way.

Temple Grandin says "it wasn't until I went to college that I realized some people are completely verbal and think only in words," and "when I invent things, I do not use language."[20] Her insights suggest imagining is a skill that differs. We play to our strengths. Yet it's not only athletes that can work on weaknesses. We're creatures of habit but need not be trapped.

Why do you choose the paths you do? How do you search for ways? Do you create options? What might it mean to change? As Nietzsche wrote "many are stubborn in pursuit of the path they have chosen, few in pursuit of the goal." The source of that quote is unknown, but to miss the truth in a lie is tragic. The will to power is naught in the absence of waypower. Or, to end differently, "the end of a melody is not its goal."[21]

Narrowing

"I imagined a labyrinth of labyrinths, of
one sinuous spreading labyrinth that
would encompass the past and the future
and in some way involve the stars."
– JORGE LUIS BORGES

The ending of our consultancy in the midst of the dotcom crash was painful. In seven years, we had grown Argus into a forty person information architecture design firm with world class clients and a global reputation. It was an amazing ride, and then abruptly I was out of work with a family to support.

Fortunately I was able to pay the bills as a freelancer while searching for a real job. Eventually I landed three interviews, information architect at IBM in Manhattan, product manager at Microsoft in Redmond, executive director of a nonprofit in Detroit, that compelled me to travel multiple divergent paths.

I flew to New York, took the train to Tarrytown to simulate the suburban commute, and learned my time at IBM would be spent mostly in meetings and email. I sat in Seattle traffic, toured real estate in the pouring rain, and fielded questions from aggressively smart people at Microsoft. I met with board members in a glassy skyscraper outside Detroit to brainstorm the conversion of philanthropic dollars into smart tech to help the urban poor. And that's when I reached my limit.

My wife and I had a house, two cars, a two year old girl, and a second daughter on the way. I could no longer afford to spend time and energy on possibility. I had to pick a path. I'd felt overwhelmed too long. In a moment of clarity, I realized that I wanted to stay in Ann Arbor and earn a living as a writer, speaker, and independent consultant. Before Claudia arrived, Semantic Studios was born. I've been on that path since 2001.

Figure 4-1. Narrowing evaluates paths and options.

While the decision was made in a moment, the narrowing took time. To compare paths emotionally, I had to travel physically. I have no regrets. But how could I? It's not possible to see past the first bend in the road not taken. In hindsight, I could have learned faster. Years later I visited a friend in Park Slope and realized I didn't need the train to Tarrytown. If I'd talked to more New Yorkers, I'd have learned about living in Brooklyn.

Drivers and Levers

The key insight of narrowing is there isn't much time. To hold open divergent paths exhausts individuals and organizations. So we must seek efficient means to identify the drivers, levers, costs, and risks that help us filter our way towards a decision.

To start we must think about search. In exploring any solution space, we may discover a path and study the steps down that path before we consider other paths. This is depth first search. It makes sense but studies show that's not how experts do it.

> Empirical studies of design planning have demonstrated that breadth-first design is associated with expert performance, while depth-first design is associated with novice performance.[1]

To illustrate, let me tell you a story. A few years ago, before Belize, I began to plan a Caribbean vacation by studying the islands. I soon fell in love with Turks & Caicos and might have spent hours finding the perfect place to stay, but I've traveled too far to make that depth first mistake. Instead I searched for flights. To my dismay, relative to nearby islands, airfare was three times more expensive. We went to St. Thomas instead.

Figure 4-2. Novice and expert search strategies.

Drivers play an outsize role in elimination of possible paths. For vacations, airfare and lodging are the usual suspects. With a wedding, it's the number of guests and budget, then venue. But in novel contexts, the variables that impact quality, cost, and time aren't clear. That's why we must search breadth first.

In the fall of junior year, to help Claire with her college search, I made a spreadsheet. She laughed at this nerd overkill. But in the winter, after a nasty bout of information anxiety, she made a spreadsheet of her own with columns for cost, location, size, and the rankings of programs in computer science and design. These drivers, paired with SAT and GPA admissions statistics, helped narrow the field for the road trip that led to a decision. The campus visits engaged Claire emotionally and helped her to prioritize the drivers. To wander and wonder is vital to the breadth first practice of narrowing. In the end, it was love at first sight. The college she chose is the place that felt like a fit.

While searching for drivers, we must also look for the levers. The Marine Corps uses "center of gravity" analysis to identify limiting factors, key variables, and vulnerabilities. I prefer the clarity of drivers and levers. Drivers support the elimination of possible paths; a college is axed due to cost, a venue is off the list as it can't hold the desired number of guests. Levers, on the other hand, open new paths and fortify existing possible paths by revealing an ability to amplify force. Finding a lever changes the answer to "if I take this path, can I make it work?"

When the Library of Congress invited me to redesign their web strategy and information architecture, I was honored and terrified. How could I make a dent? The answers I found were three levers – portals, search, objects – that let us make change by working top-down and bottom-up with search as the glue.[2] This matters because the structure of software and websites is more potent than we know. These places made of information are levers. We shape our rectangles; thereafter they shape us.[3]

Levers are integral to systems thinking and may not work as we expect. Prohibition in the 1920s abetted organized crime, as does our modern war on drugs. Blowback and backlash often deliver the opposite of intent. To not be blindsided by second order effects, before you pull a lever, look at least a step ahead.

As parents we learn the levers change with time. Lately, the path to attention runs through the phone and car keys. Take those away, and we get our teenager back. Levers are small things that make all the difference between a viable path and a dead end. Are there levers that can open paths to your goals?

Estimates and Risk

To filter paths, estimates are the tool we rely on most, despite the fact they are usually wrong. How long will it take? What will it cost? It's wise to question the answers. A fair number of estimating failures are spectacular. The Sydney Opera House was approved as a 4 year $7 million project but took 14 years and $102 million. Dean Kamen estimated Segway would sell 10,000 units a week, and investor John Doerr forecast it would reach $1 billion in sales faster than any company in history. Six years later, only 30,000 had been built, and they later sold the firm at a loss. Of course, most of our mistakes are mundane. We're late for a meeting due to traffic. The sales forecast is off due to weather. The budget is blown by a broken furnace. We make estimates every day. The small ones are usually good enough. It's the ones with major consequences we get wrong.

The first step to recovery is awareness of the planning fallacy. Studies by Daniel Kahneman and Amos Tversky reveal our estimates display an optimism bias.[4] When asked how long it will take, we predictably underestimate. Of course, that's only when pondering our own tasks. Outsiders err the other way.

We must also be aware of perverse incentives and conflicts of interest. If we or those we ask are motivated to miscalculate, estimates can swing high or low. That said, it's not a bad idea to ask an expert who knows the usual times, costs, and pitfalls. Also, it helps to ask peers. Get independent estimates, and then discuss differences as a group. From the Delphi method to prediction markets, many estimates are better than one.

A proven way to boost accuracy is to break tasks into subtasks and estimate each one. The sum of the parts tends to be greater than the original estimate of the whole. If timely completion is a priority, it pays to map the critical path. List all tasks and the time each will take. Then, identify dependencies, noting tasks that must occur in sequence and tasks that can run in parallel.

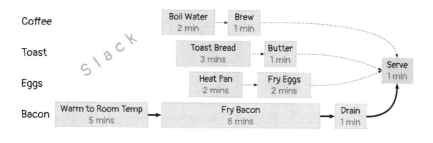

Figure 4-3. Critical path on a Gantt chart.

The critical path is the longest path and often has zero slack. If any task on that path is delayed, the project will be late. Let's say you have 15 minutes to cook breakfast. The critical path is made of bacon. If you forget to remove it from the fridge first, breakfast will be late, unless you're willing to risk quality by frying it cold or using the microwave.[5] It's overkill to make a Gantt chart for breakfast, but to be on time, it always helps to be aware of the critical path, and to add slack when possible.

Risk is the reason to include slack in the critical path, and risk assessment plays a huge role in narrowing. Of course, as bad as we are at estimates, we're far worse at evaluating risk. "What could possibly go wrong?" is a question we can never fully answer and rarely dare to ask. Intentional interactions with uncertainty are uncomfortable. Faced with potential for gain or loss, we cross our fingers instead of rolling up sleeves.

Risk illiteracy leads to bad decisions. In the wake of 9/11, fear led many Americans to drive rather than fly, resulting in 1,600 indirect, additional deaths due to the terrorist attack. Statistics tell us it's far safer to fly, but we can't feel the numbers. As risk expert Gerd Gigerenzer explains, we tend to trust our gut.

> My research with managers suggests that the higher up they are in the hierarchy, the greater their reliance on gut feelings. Yet most said that when they have to justify decisions to third parties, they hide their intuition and look for reasons after the fact.[6]

Emotion can help us to make wise decisions, but only if we're more careful in what we feed our gut. Part of the problem is probability. When a meteorologist predicts a 20 percent chance of rain, do we even know what that means? Is it that on 1 of 5 days for which this prediction is made, .01 inches will fall? Is it an average across the area? In my experience it means that if I go for a bike ride, there's a 100 percent chance I'll get soaked.

We also get risk wrong by failing to admit uncertainty. If asked to speak at an event in Paris, I may plan to arrive a day early to allow for delays. But this risk mitigation would have failed in 2010 when the volcanic eruption of Eyjafjallajökull caused the largest air traffic shutdown since World War II. Uncertainty outnumbers probability. As I often tell my wife, it's what you're not worrying about that will get you.

Fortunately, we can use risk literacy to select and shape better paths. We might begin by translating probabilities into natural frequencies. For instance, evidence that mammograms reduce a woman's chance of dying from breast cancer by 20 percent translates to an absolute risk reduction of 1 in 1,000. Also, it's vital to find the right frame. If you expand the scope to death from all cancers, there's no evidence mammograms save lives. Screenings add risks. False alarms may lead to anxiety and needless interventions with serious consequences. Mitigation as Taleb writes in *The Black Swan* is often the best we can do.

> This idea that in order to make a decision you need to focus on the consequences (which you can know) rather than the probability (which you can't know) is the central idea of uncertainty.[7]

Let's say I worry about that invite to speak in Paris. I could limit my liability with an "act of god" clause in the contract, stating the organizer covers airfare if I miss the event due to illness or natural disaster. Before I accept, I might also think about opportunity cost. What if I get a better offer? We rarely get to see all paths at once. Even if I can cancel at no cost, will I feel guilt? Risk is an element we can accept, avoid, mitigate, or transfer. To select a path of wisdom, it helps to be self aware.

Of course, as we can't see past the first bend in any path, it's often wise to retain options. In project management, risk falls as the "cone of uncertainty" tapers. In Agile, choices are made at the "last responsible moment." And in the halls of Amazon, folks lean into decisions that are reversible "two-way doors."

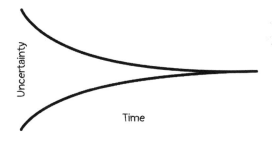

Figure 4-4. Cone of uncertainty.

Options are good, but as Niels Bohr told Einstein in a debate on quantum physics "opposites are complementary" and the opposite of a profound truth may well be a profound truth.[8] Barry Schwartz maps this to planning in *The Paradox of Choice*.

> We are enamored of freedom, self-determination, and variety, and are reluctant to give up any of our options. But clinging tenaciously to all the choices available to us contributes to bad decisions, to anxiety, stress, and dissatisfaction – even clinical depression.[9]

Options are traps. Two-way doors are heavier than we think. We are sad and indecisive when forced to confront tradeoffs. If you struggle with a decision, to irrevocably commit is one way to relief. The opposite truth is the wisdom of burning bridges.

It can also help to not know. There are times when it's simply best to act, not ask. A successful entrepreneur once told me "if I'd known then what I know now, I'd never have begun."

We travel one path in life. The labyrinth we walk is our story. But our futures are divergent. We face a maze of hidden paths with infinite possibility, a prospect that can inspire and terrify us all. Jorge Luis Borges calls it the garden of forking paths.

Figure 4-5. The labyrinth and the maze.

We have free will. In this garden, we must find our own way. But we can't make good decisions if overwhelmed by options. Too often we pick a path in haste based on fear or false belief. That's why narrowing matters. To look for levers and drivers and evaluate estimates and risks is an efficient way to filter options to reach a decision set your mind and gut can digest.

Principles to Practices

To involve our mnemonic, let's make narrowing more social by asking for help. Pioneers may tell where they went wrong.

Experts can identify drivers and levers. Peers can help us rank paths and list pros and cons. If negotiation will be necessary, start to talk; resistance may be a signal to eliminate that path.

Together with Gantt charts, three point estimation can make schedule risk tangible. For each task, capture an optimistic, pessimistic, and most likely time it will take. You can create a weighted average to allow for uncertainty, but simply writing the numbers makes the point. A risk matrix makes tangible the interaction of probability and consequence. Start a register and then map to a matrix to highlight the risks that merit attention.

Risk	Impact	Odds	Weight
Flight Delay	1	4	4
Winter Blizzard	3	2	6
Icelandic Volcano	5	.05	.25

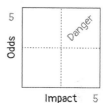

Figure 4-6. Risk matrix.

To make estimating social, tangible, and agile, play planning poker. Buy or build a deck with Fibonacci numbers or grab a mobile app. Describe a task. Then each individual lays a card face down. The number on the card is their estimate. Flip the cards and discuss differences. Repeat until consensus. The estimates are in points, not minutes. Relative sizing of tasks makes it easy to adjust schedules later. If a team plays often and learns from experience, estimates will be more accurate.

In colonial India, the British tried to reduce the number of venomous snakes in Delhi by paying cash for dead cobras. It worked for a while until people began breeding cobras, then the government killed the bounty, and breeders set their snakes free. Reflect on the exposure of your plan to the cobra effect. Is it possible you'll achieve the opposite of your goals?

To reflect, map the system, then map the context outside the system; that's where surprises come from. Or sketch the pace layers from fast to slow, then add drivers and levers; those that are deep are powerful but hard to move. After a project in a debrief ask the team to sort surprises into three categories: what we didn't know, what we couldn't know, what we didn't want to know; and then ask why. Before a project, consider emotion in defining task order. Use a few quick wins to build momentum, then tackle the scary tasks early, so anxiety can't drag you down. Finally, go for a walk or take a nap, since we tend to choose better paths better when we're in a good mood.

Deciding

*"Bind me as I stand upright, with a bond
so fast that I cannot possibly break away."*
– ULYSSES

I ran the Boston Marathon. That's why we do it. To say those
five words. In running circles, qualifying for this race affords
bragging rights. And I must confess ego gratification was one
of my goals. But the race didn't go according to plan. I began
fast and felt good through the Wellesley Scream Tunnel, but
by mile 20 it was my knees that were screaming, and I feared
I'd fail to finish. So, for the first time ever in a race, I walked.
Up Heartbreak Hill and under the persistent stare of the iconic
Citgo Sign, I walked past thousands of fans, whilst thousands
of runners passed me. It was a difficult, chastening experience.

I didn't train well due to hubris, low motivation, ignorance of
the impact of hills on knees, and there's one more thing. It was
a truly bad Michigan winter. A polar vortex sent temperatures
far below zero for weeks, and due to snow there was only one

place to run long distances, a park with a plowed 3 mile loop. This meant I had to decide, again and again, not to quit.

Often, broken by ice wind, I'd quit, only to decide to run on at the end of a loop. I was miserable, ran slow, and cut mileage. I longed for an out and back, to slip the commits of this infinite loop. Running is the easy part. It's deciding to run that's hard.

Figure 5-1. Deciding means committing to a belief, path, or goal.

Decisions can be private. You set your mind or take the first step. Decisions can be public. You make a promise or sign a contract. Also, choices can be singular or shared. I change my mind. We agree to a plan. It matters who's the decider, since commitments yield consequences in blood, toil, and tears. We must take responsibility for our decisions, so it pays to make them timely and well, neither too soon, late, fixed, nor flexible.

Before we commit, it helps to look ahead. A plan is a design or map used to render intent or reach a goal. As time travel tools, plans let us explore, understand, persuade, and specify before a decision. A sketch shows vision. A scientific method details materials, conditions, and steps. Next are metrics. What counts as success? How might we know if we chose the right path?

Logic and Emotion

In college I took a class on rational choice in which we learned to make decision trees. As models of paths, probabilities, and consequences, these forking graphs spin options into numbers.

To begin, draw the root decision as a square, and a branch for each possible path. Use circles for chances with probabilities. Add squares and circles as needed, then an endpoint triangle. List costs and rewards. Last, calculate the value of each plan.

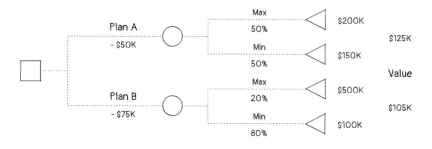

Figure 5-2. Decision tree.

If it sounds easy, it's not. Try to model a real decision as a tree, and you'll see what I mean. And if it makes sense, it doesn't. I mean it's useful as a guide but don't use trees to make choices, as behind their statistical veneer, these trees are seriously silly.

To start, people aren't rational. In the words of Herbert Simon, at best we satisfice under conditions of bounded rationality.[1] Given limited time, information, and intelligence, we use rules of thumb or heuristics to make choices that are good enough.

In truth, many choices are worse than good enough. Studies of decision making under risk reveal our behavior is inconsistent with utility theory. As Kahneman and Tversky argue in their paper on prospect theory, "people underweight outcomes that are merely probable in comparison with outcomes that are obtained with certainty (which contributes to) risk aversion in choices involving sure gains and to risk seeking in choices involving sure losses."[2] So we have insurance and gambling.

It gets worse. Basing studies of chance on the narrow world of games and dice is ludicrous. Nassim Taleb argues the misuse of games to model life is a "ludic fallacy" as the real world is infinitely more complex. We can't use math to solve for reality, and we face wicked problems far more than we dare to admit.

It gets worse. If the Wikipedia list of cognitive biases fails to convince you that we all suffer from *dysrationalia*, the inability to think and act rationally despite adequate intelligence, that's because you're blinded by confirmation and hindsight bias.

Seriously, the best answer to our faults is a sense of humor, the sum of logic and emotion, and hope. In the face of uncertainty, irrationality, misinformation, incompatible goals, and fear, we get to make inspired decisions. The solution to life is gratitude. Sure, it's easy to follow orders or the herd or to obey authority and the algorithms, but isn't it more fun to go your own way?

My first marathon went much better than my last. I ran Detroit the year I turned 40, and I was a man with a plan. My goal was to qualify for Boston at the 18-34 age group pace. My younger brother said I couldn't do it, so I was motivated. I used a GPS watch and 16 week scientific program to train less, run faster.[3] I've never worked so hard in my life. At times I feared injury. One misstep, a torn tendon, and my run would end. The way I lost my fear was to laugh at the absurdity of it all. It's crazy to run 26.2 miles at a 7:15 pace, and I'm so lucky I get to try. In the end, it took grit, and I did it. To run is not a choice I regret.

Of course, regret is full of bias. Garry Kasparov asks people to think of the last time they made a bad decision, and most folks simply cannot. He says we decide like we talk, unconsciously, and to improve we must be far more reflective and self-aware.

What bad habits have you picked up in your decision making? Which steps do you skip and which do you overemphasize? Do your poor decisions tend to stem from bad information, poor evaluation, incorrect calculation, or a combination of these?[4]

Before asking if we made the right choice at the right time, we might ask if we were the right ones to choose. Micromanagers make decisions they shouldn't, but rarely see things that way. But how can we judge the decisions we do make? Did we use a vivid frame, imagine diverse paths, find good data, identify values and tradeoffs, and temper logic with emotion? Process is worthy of measure, but Scott McNealy makes a good point.

> It's important to make good decisions. But I spend much less time and energy worrying about 'making the right decision' and more time and energy ensuring that any decision I make turns out right.[5]

Execution is vital to success, and a good team can save a bad plan. On the other hand, there are variables out of our control, and plans that predictably fail. But we rarely take credit for a bad outcome. We say "it's not my fault." Or memory is edited by *choice supportive bias*, and we say "it's not so bad after all."

Maps and Plans

Metrics are a tool we use to keep ourselves honest. If we agree to a numeric definition of success, we leave no wiggle room. I either hit my numbers, or I don't. Organizations love targets for their clarity. Objectives and key results, key performance indicators, and net promoter scores are in fashion today, but metrics are not new, and neither are the problems they cause.

> People with targets and jobs dependent upon meeting them will probably meet the targets, even if they have to destroy the enterprise to do it.

This quote by W. Edwards Deming is apocryphal, but the source is less significant than its popularity. We all know the dark side of metrics, but we use them anyway. In my work with large organizations, I see the damage they cause all the time. I do believe there's a better way, but we must learn to look before we leap, as Eric Ries explains in *The Lean Startup*.

> A true experiment follows the scientific method. It begins with a clear hypothesis that makes predictions about what is supposed to happen. It then tests those predictions empirically.[6]

Before deciding on a path, we must form a hypothesis, make predictions, and design tests. If we can't define ways to learn from feedback, it may not be the right path. The vanity metrics we advertise regularly do more harm than good, but if we can define actionable metrics in advance, they may help us decide. But we must be wary of numbers as incentives. To see the *why* behind the *what* requires qualitative and quantitative methods, and awareness that metrics are but signals of goals and intent.

I walked the Boston Marathon. Years later, to write those five words, it hurts. Did I make a bad decision? Perhaps. I entered to collect my medal. I didn't plan for bad weather or big hills. My heart wasn't in it. But I also entered for the experience. It was an honor to be part of the world's oldest marathon, and to share the day with family was a joy I won't forget. It's hard to recall a bad decision, because we change day by day. But you can decide more wisely, as where there's a will there's a way.

A plan can multiply willpower and waypower, and may also help us to choose. While we often make plans after a decision, to render intent before can lead us down the right path. Plans exist on a *why* to *how* spectrum. We use a sketch to grow the will and steps to show the way. A model or prototype makes the goal bigger, so we feel a twinge of success and know *why* to try. Maps show the way, so we know *how* to get there from here. Recipes mix ingredients and directions with photos to lure us down a path: see this cake; imagine how good it tastes.

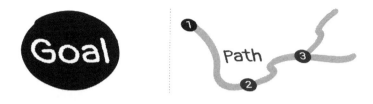

Figure 5-3. Plans exist on a why to how spectrum.

To plan is to wonder before we wander. Or a plan might be to persuade or control. Plans vary in purpose and complexity. The simplest artifact is a list. It lets us distribute cognition, so we can think better, manage instructions, and recall our intent.

We use instructions every day, but they are often out of order, so Richard Saul Wurman wrote *Follow the Yellow Brick Road*.

> I know a man who taught his son to tie his shoe in five minutes. He tied the shoelace into a bow, then untied it one step at a time. He taught his son by doing it backwards. His son instantly grasped the relationship of each step to the tied bow. He showed his son the goal (the bow), then showed him the steps leading up to the goal.[7]

For a writer, it's natural to start with step one, but the opposite may be true for the reader. Wurman invites us to question the structure of instructions. Before process and schedule, define mission and destination. Help folks to anticipate forks in the road. Describe both conditions of success and failure. Why will I do this? Where am I going? What are the signs I'm not lost? How long will it take? How do I know I've gone too far?

The Marines use a similar recipe to prepare an order. A plan should balance guidance with freedom, state not just steps but intent, and mix graphic with narrative form. And the Marines realize that "when writing plans or orders, words matter." To defeat is not to destroy. Also, as attention is scarce in war and peace, "a good order is judged on its usefulness, not its size."[8]

In deciding, order matters too. The act of writing instructions can help us to evaluate plans *before* we make a decision. As we explain steps, we may uncover costs and risks, especially if we use empathy to bridge time, space, and multiple perspectives.

Plans are axiomatic in the work I do. The maps that precede a project include my list of services, a proposal or scope of work, and a contract. Plans as deliverables include experience maps, ontologies, wireframes, and prototypes. And my projects end with a planning workshop to collaboratively build a roadmap. This recipe includes an inspiring, achievable vision and tools for judicious deciding and executing. Measure twice, cut once.

There's a mental disorder, aboulomania, in which the patient displays pathological indecisiveness. Our friends who can never decide what to order at a restaurant are clearly on the spectrum. To be fair, we all suffer iffiness and vacillation. We may be so overwhelmed or ambivalent, we choose to decide through inaction. Or we commit to a diet only to gobble junk food the same day. Donuts are delicious. Resolution is tough.

Words are one way out. We can make a promise, swear an oath, or state our intent in a tweet. In voicing a decision, we enlist others in support, and make it hard to retreat. That's what Winston Churchill did by speaking irrevocable words.

> We shall fight on the beaches, we shall fight on the landing grounds, we shall fight in the fields and in the streets, we shall fight in the hills; we shall never surrender.[9]

Of course, to act makes it even harder to retract. Julius Caesar crossed the Rubicon precisely *because* there was no going back. The Roman Empire was built by strategically burning bridges. Stranded troops are given no choice but to fight for their lives.

In modern times, we trap ourselves with software, contracts, architecture, laws, culture, governance, and process. We bury decisions in frameworks to limit rights and action. We seek future control via living wills or relax it by power of attorney.

A Ulysses Pact is a tool I use to bind my future self. Before I train for a marathon or try to lose weight, I sign a contract to limit what I eat and drink, stipulating that if I break it, I must donate $50 to a cause I despise. My family serve as witnesses and wardens. I don't use it often, but when I do, it works.

The origin of this pact is Odysseus who told his sailors to bind him to the mast, so he could listen to but not be lured by the Sirens. In translation from Greek to Roman, Odysseus became Ulysses, and in the parallax shift to Irish, James Joyce rewrote the hero as an everyman suffering compassion, introspection, indecision, and remorse. The point is deciding is cultural. The plans of Odysseus are subject to Gods, destiny, and tradition, whereas the right choice in Ulysses is a matter of perspective.

In Ulysses, the word "parallax" occurs seven times. Parallax is the apparent displacement of an object due to a change in the position or line of sight of the observer. Astronomers use it to calculate the distance of stars. We see it when we hold up one thumb, and peer through one eye, then the other. Joyce uses it to make a point. A decision is judged in the eye of a beholder.

Principles to Practices

The first point in our star is social. How can we include folks in the practice of deciding? A promise is a commitment to do or not do something. Less than a contract, more than a maybe, it's not a bad place to start. A charrette engages stakeholders in an intense period of planning or design. As a way to decide that adds perspectives and buy-in, it can lead to a better end.

A list of pros and cons is decidedly tangible, but perhaps add emotion as well. How do you expect to feel at the end of each path, and how long do you think it will last? In organizations, a RACI matrix that notes who is responsible and accountable and who must be consulted or informed can guide decisions and communications for each task. To organize project tasks, roles, scope, and schedule, a work breakdown structure (WBS) is the time tested choice. If you want to go modern, try Trello. I know an executive who uses it to micromanage his business and palatial estate. He has a Trello board with instructions for how to wash his Ferrari and not scratch the paint. As mobile apps enable remote control, they may change what we decide.

Agility is made with metrics and two-way doors. What are the leading indicators? How early can we get feedback? If we turn back or pivot, what's the cost? Also, we hold options when we procrastinate. A timeline with milestones for earliest possible decision, last responsible moment, and point of no return can help us see when to choose. Again, tools can change the map.

Figure 5-4. Decision timeline.

A friend was in a wedding choreographed with Google Sheets. The bride organized the event precisely by person, task, space, and time. It's a stunning artifact. There are numbers in case of emergency, lists so it's impossible to forget, and mobile so it's never too late. Rough and risky territory is tamed by the likes of Google Maps. The same is true when we travel. Why select a restaurant until you're hungry? Algorithms will choose the way. Technology lets us decide differently, and often not at all.

Flipism means to make all decisions by flipping a coin. It is a silly idea with a serious point. We can never truly predict the consequences of our actions. Oddly, in the face of uncertainty, it may help to flip a coin, roll the dice, turn a magic 8-ball, or ask the Ouija board. If you get the right or wrong answer, the body may speak with a twinge of a wisdom older than words.

Figure 5-5. Styles of decision making.

To reflect on rationality, catalog the biases that may be at play, and list the pros and cons of your style in relation to the choice you must make. Go for a walk, try yoga, get rest, because how you've always decided may not be best. Reflect on the insight of Ulysses: habits are ties that bind and tradition isn't all good.

Executing

*"There was one of two things I had a right
to, liberty or death; if I could not have one,
I would have the other."*

– HARRIET TUBMAN

The day after I failed Longs Peak the second time, I decided to climb Mount Ida. I hoped for the predawn rain in Estes Park to burst into sunshine on the 25 mile drive to Milner Pass. As my Ford Mustang rose in the high country, so did my spirits. And then I realized my mistake. I have lived all my life in flatlands. I'm not used to being mile high. As rain turned to snow, road turned to ice, and I had no way to turn back. I drove slow on Trail Ridge, the land's highest road, through serpentine twists with sheer drops, no guardrails, yet my pony car chose to fishtail. My blood ran as cold as the black ice under my tires.

A mile and a lifetime later, I pulled into a deserted pit stop, a place to wait out the storm. A few folks went by with hardier cars than I. An hour went by, a park ranger drove up, told me the road's closed, I had to go back. But the sun was up, the ice was melting, I drove down safely, and that's the point. I failed Mount Ida, but some goals are more vital than others. A lesson I've learned in life is patience. In my youth, I'd have driven on.

To execute is "to carry out a plan," but the dichotomy between do and plan is false. To act or drive responsively, we also plan as we go. We listen to feedback, learn from disruption, and opt to pivot or persist. We must dance to discover our steps. Either path takes grit or *spirit* which recalls the why to light the way.

Figure 6-1. Executing is the improv dance of listen, learn, and lead.

Pivot or Persist

The dream of Agile is the synthesis of execution and planning in software creation. If we plan together at the last responsible moment, we allow for progressive elaboration to continuously improve a plan with more accurate information and estimates. The product backlog in Scrum is a list of things to be done for the project. In an iterative series of sprints, the team tackles a subset of that list based on up to date priorities and estimates. A daily standup drives feedback and edits to the plan. It's not easy to pull off due to old habits, people, and culture, but this recipe for planning while executing includes fresh ingredients.

The same is true for Lean. From manufacturing to startups, to frame execution as experiment allows incremental planning to improve the chances for success. Minimum viable products and small batches drive validated learning. Early detection of truth and error lets us pivot faster yet deciding on the fly isn't easy. As Eric Ries testifies, it's the hardest thing we do.

> Upon completing the Build-Measure-Learn loop, we confront the most difficult question any entrepreneur faces: whether to pivot the original strategy or persevere.[1]

YouTube began as a video dating site. Twitter was a platform for podcasts. Nintendo sold playing cards and ran love hotels before the pivot to video games. In hindsight the right path is obvious, but that's not true at the time. The team is invested in the original vision and stuck in a sunk cost trap. Also, there's no path after a pivot. It's scary to go off the map. The deciding is done while executing, as there's no time to put a company on hold. It's easier to persevere, and that's what we mostly do.

In the 1990s, as a young CEO of a growing consulting firm, I was busy. I loved days with 8+ meetings, but it was stressful too. If defining information architecture while learning to run a business was a juggling act, I dropped more than one ball. The biggest errors were in delegation. To micromanage isn't good, but hiring, firing, and check signing are duties a small business owner should not cede. I also failed to hear and act upon grievances that had the power to damage our culture. In hindsight I'd do things differently, but that's because I've had time to reflect. In the heat of the moment, there's no time, or at least that's how it feels. In reality, we can pull off to the side of the road and take breaks. Also, we might learn to be mindful.

Thich Nhat Hanh says mindfulness can penetrate the activity of everyday life, each minute, each hour, and not just describe something far away.[2] This is the promise of meditation and yoga, but in the mess of modernity, it's a hard one to fulfill.

It won't get easier. In our era, the rate of change in all the pace layers – *fashion, commerce, infrastructure, governance, culture, and nature* – is faster than what normal used to be. Sustainable energy, space colonization, gene editing, artificial intelligence, and autonomous drones are on the way, even as we struggle with truth, ethics, authority, democracy, trust and the Internet.

Amazon is striking in feats and flaws. Prime Now delivers in two hours or less, so you can order everything from breakfast to diapers in bed. But I've seen this brand fail to deliver on its promise, as two day shipping slips to three days or not at all. A book I ordered recently was delivered a day late by a perfect stranger. The postal service left it at the wrong address. Worse are the times Track Package says my order has arrived, but it's not here. Sadly Amazon offers no way to report a gap between their system and reality. Why would a firm with a "relentless customer focus" fail to design for feedback? People who don't listen can't learn. You might think Jeff Bezos would know that.

Of course, even a great leader can become the limiting factor if they fail to decentralize control. In Iraq in 2003, after realizing conventional tactics were failing, General Stanley McChrystal used this insight to turn the tables on al-Qaeda. Command and control was too slow to fight a shapeshifting terrorist network. Noting it was not a war of planning and discipline, but one of agility and innovation, and "planning was predicated on our ability to predict; which we couldn't,"[3] McChrystal decided to pivot towards the radical new goal of shared consciousness.

> Effective prediction has become increasingly difficult, and in many situations impossible. Continuing to function under the illusion that we can understand and foresee exactly what will be relevant to whom is hubris. It might feel safe, but it is the opposite.

> Functioning safely in an interdependent environment requires that every team possess a holistic understanding of the interaction between all the moving parts. Everyone has to see the system in its entirety for the plan to work.[4]

To break down silos, he tore down walls, from the redesign of physical workspaces to the transformation of communications.

> My command team and I added people to the cc line of emails whenever it seemed even the second or third order consequence of the operation discussed might impact them. We had to acknowledge we often could not predict who would and would not benefit from access to certain information. We took almost all phone calls on speakerphone: that included me, the commander in charge of our nation's most sensitive forces. This could make people uncomfortable, sometimes intensely so. But never once did I see it hurt us as much as it helped. We were trying to normalize sharing among people used to the opposite. Our standing guidance was 'share information until you're afraid it's illegal.'[5]

And this plan for improvisation did work. His team of teams beat back al-Qaeda. In the fog of war, McChrystal was able to see the flaw in how we always do things. A career solider who graduated West Point in 1976, this old dog used new tricks to win. As Louis Pasteur said, chance favors the prepared mind.

Gary Klein knows the value of experience in decision making under duress. His observations of firefighters, battle planners, critical care nurses, pilots, and nuclear power plant operators show "recognition-primed decision strategy" to be the norm.[6] In the fog of war experts are able to understand patterns and shift paths and goals with no map or sign to say *You Are Here*.

Klein makes a vital distinction stating "intuition is the use of patterns already learned, whereas insight is the discovery of new patterns."[7] Experts gain insights by seeing connections, coincidences, curiosities, and contradictions others miss, but they can also be trapped by overconfidence in flawed beliefs, which makes it tough to pivot. A goal insight is hardest of all. Many of us change paths, but we rarely dare change the goal.

Spirit

Our culture celebrates grit. It's no surprise we stay the course. There's even a *Grit* book that tells how such high achievers as Michael Phelps, Jeff Bezos, and Jamie Dimon blended passion and perseverance to succeed. Consider, for example, the story of Steve Young, legendary quarterback of San Francisco 49ers and MVP of Super Bowl XXIX. Steve credits the tough love of his father as vital to his success. At age 13, after a long season of failure and humiliation, Steve decided to quit, but "My dad looked me straight in the eye and said 'You cannot quit. You have the ability, so you need to go back and work this out.'"[8] Later, at Brigham Young University, as a freshman and eighth string quarterback, lonely and miserable, Steve wanted to quit and come home, but that was unacceptable to his father.

> You can quit, but you can't come home, because I'm not going to live with a quitter. You've known that since you were a kid.[9]

But wait. Is this story inspiring or disturbing? Clearly grit can be valuable. Mastery demands willpower, a growth mindset, deliberate practice, courage, and 10,000 hours. But if it means never quit or question goals, grit may be bad for your health.

I'm fairly gritty by nature. I select challenges cautiously, but once in, I rarely back out. You can't complete two marathons and an Ironman 70.3 triathlon or write six books without grit. But that doesn't mean I don't quit. In addition to mountainous turnabouts, I've closed a business and stopped eating animals. It takes courage to quit, and I'm not afraid to change my mind.

Grit can be a grind, so I aim for spirit. There are times we must stay, suffer, endure, but a mindset of gratitude and joy is more likely to succeed. Spirit recalls purpose and meaning. Why am I doing this? It reminds us we're lucky we get to try. If I stress too long, I feel the pain in my body. But if my vision and goals are solid and spirits are high, I feel free to write or run forever.

Harriet Tubman was born a slave. At the hands of oppressors she suffered the whip and severe head injury before deciding to run for freedom, forever binding herself to liberty or death.

> If you hear the dogs, keep going. If you see the torches in the woods, keep going. If there's shouting after you, keep going. Don't ever stop. Keep going. If you want a taste of freedom, keep going.

This quote is apocryphal. The words are not hers. But in spirit, these lines ring true. Two brothers fled with her, but turned back in fear, leaving 20-25 year old Harriet alone in the dark.

> And so, with only the North Star for her guide, our heroine started on the way to liberty. 'For I had reasoned dis out in my mind; there was one of two things I had a right to, liberty or death; if I could not have one, I would have de oder; for no man should take me alive; I should fight for my liberty as long as my strength lasted.'[10]

Harriet fled the South, then boldly went back. As a conductor on the Underground Railroad, she made the 80 mile journey 19 times and freed 300 slaves. She served the Union Army in the Civil War as a nurse, cook, and scout. Later she founded a home for aged and indigent colored people, and spoke up for the women's right to vote. As a slave, she "used to dream of flying over fields, towns, rivers, and mountains, looking down upon them like a bird, reaching at last a great fence or river,"[11] and that perhaps is the secret to her success. Harriet endured because she had true vision and purpose. William H. Seward, Secretary of State under President Lincoln, knew this well.

> I have known Harriet long, and a nobler, higher spirit, or a truer, seldom dwells in human form.[12]

She was shrewd in planning. John Brown relied on her skill for military strategy. He called her General Tubman. But Harriet is best known for perseverance. We all have conflicting goals, but she understood the power of a top goal to organize a life. Her faith we are created equal lifted her spirit and lit the way. Liberty and justice for all was her North Star. What's yours?

Principles to Practices

To make executing social, it helps to have a team. For those who are so blessed, family dinner is a daily ritual that affords a chance to share updates, insights, and feedback. At work we may use Twitter or Slack as a new water cooler, but the killer app remains a diverse team with shared goals. If a black swan blocks your path, the parallax of investors, advisors, and peers with different backgrounds, beliefs and perspectives will find a way around. Diversity is a cure for unpredictable adversity.

Figure 6-2. Diversity offers a different angle.

Years ago, we took the girls skiing. Claire was just old enough to be in charge of her own suitcase. The trip was fun, but after a long drive home, we discovered her case to be nearly empty. She'd hidden (unpacked) her clothes in a chest of drawers. My wife rang the hotel, while I used this teachable moment to tell the girls how to "make it impossible to forget" with a tangible reminder you can't ignore. Sticky notes on doors and a string around a finger are okay, but I leave clothes in a visible place.

Kanban makes executing social, tangible, and agile. To move tasks publicly left to right – to do, doing, done – on the board invites shared consciousness. A burn down or burn up chart does that too; up is more agile as it affords changes to scope.

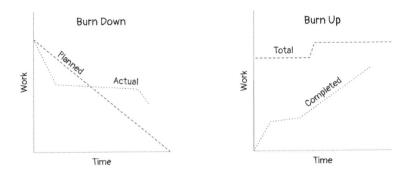

Figure 6-3. Burn down and burn up charts.

In 1998 I managed the most stressful project of my life. Our team was working 16 hour days when our client demanded we meet face to face. I flew to New Jersey, and all I recall is our client, a grizzly bear of a man, screaming at the top of his lungs. In the aftershock, I learned our work was fine, and we were on time, it was my email that was the problem. I'd been so busy, I'd failed to reply swiftly, so he thought I didn't care. I learned the hard way for communication there's always time. It's not only that people assume the worst but also feedback is useless without attention. People who don't listen won't pivot.

To be reflective play with time. To design "slack" or time for low priority tasks at the end of a sprint into a plan can work, but I prefer an early deadline. As a conductor once noted "to achieve great things, two things are needed, a plan and not quite enough time."[13] The genius of a 12 week year rests in the dance of possible and urgent. Rhythm helps too. Use a weekly power hour with a spiral bound planner to reflect on lessons learned and what's next. Map OODA loops to your territory. Sketch the cycle by which you observe, orient, decide, and act, and identify possible sources of error. Tempo in a loop is key, but mindful matters too. To be aware is to prepare. Disruption is easy to ignore. Pull to the side of the road. You have time. In deciding to pivot or persist, use a shorter iteration of FINDER.

Fall seven times, rise eight. The Japanese proverb instructs us to persevere, keep going, be resilient. In the face of adversity, execute the plan. But is that all? Folks in our society argue the math. We must rise more than fall as we start in dust. I prefer a different ending to this kōan. Perhaps step eight is different. Our body rises to stand, then the spirit rises in enlightenment. The work of life is freedom when the right star lights the way.

Reflecting

"Can machines think?"
– ALAN TURING

Once upon a time, there was a happy family. Every night at dinner, mom, dad, and two girls who still believed in Santa played a game. The rules are simple. Tell three stories about your day, two true, one false, and see who can detect the fib. Today I saw a lady walk a rabbit on a leash. Today I found a tooth in the kitchen. Today I forgot my underwear. The family ate, laughed, and learned together, and lied happily ever after.

There's truth in the tale. It's mostly not false. We did play this game, for years, and it was fun. We loved to stun and bewilder each other, yet the big surprise was insight. In reflecting on my day, I was often amazed by oddities already lost. If not for the intentional search for anomaly, I'd have erased these standard deviations from memory. The misfits we find, we rarely recall.

We observe a tiny bit of reality. We understand and remember even less. Unlike most machines, our memory is selective and purposeful. Goals and beliefs define what we notice and store.

To mental maps we add places we predict we'll need to visit later. It's not about the past. The intent of memory is to plan.

In reflecting we look back to go forward. We search the past for truths and insights to shift the future. I'm not speaking of nostalgia, though we are all borne back ceaselessly and want what we think we had. My aim is redirection. In reflecting on inconvenient truths, I hope to change not only paths but goals.

Figure 7-1. Reflection changes direction.

We all have times for reflection. Alone in the shower or on a walk, we retrace the steps of a day. Together at lunch for work or over family dinner, we share memories and missteps. Some of us reflect more rigorously than others. Given time, it shows.

> People who as a matter of habit extract underlying principles or rules from new experiences are more successful learners than those who take their experiences at face value, failing to infer lessons that can be applied later in similar situations.[1]

In Agile, the sprint retrospective offers a collaborative context for reflection. Every two to four weeks, at the end of a sprint, the team meets for an hour or so to look back. Focal questions include 1) what went well? 2) what went wrong? 3) how might we improve? In reflecting on the plan, execution, and results, the team explores surprises, conflicts, roadblocks, and lessons.

In addition to conventional analysis, a retrospective creates an opportunity for double loop learning. To edit planned actions based on feedback is normal, but revising assumptions, goals, values, methods, or metrics may effect change more profound. A team able to expand the frame may hack their habits, beliefs, and environment to be better prepared to succeed and learn.

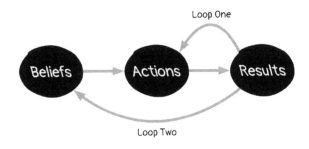

Figure 7-2. Double loop learning.

Retrospectives allow for constructive feedback to drive team learning and bonding, but that's what makes them hard. We may lack courage to be honest, and often people can't handle the truth. Our filters are as powerful as they are idiosyncratic, which means we're all blind men touching a tortoise, or is it a tree or an elephant? It hurts to reconcile different perceptions of reality, so all too often we simply shut up and shut down.

Search for Truth

To seek truth together requires a culture of humility and respect. We are all deeply flawed and valuable. We must all speak and listen. Ideas we don't implement may lead to those we do. Errors we find aren't about fault, since our intent is a future fix. And counterfactuals merit no more confidence than predictions, as we never know what would have happened if.

Reflection is more fruitful if we know our own minds, but that is harder than we think. An imperfect ability to predict actions of sentient beings is a product of evolution. It's quick and dirty yet better than nothing in the context of survival in a jungle or a tribe. Intriguingly, cognitive psychology and neuroscience have shown we use the same *theory of mind* to study ourselves.

> Self-awareness is just this same mind reading ability, turned around and employed on our own mind, with all the fallibility, speculation, and lack of direct evidence that bedevils mind reading as a tool for guessing at the thought and behavior of others.[2]

Empirical science tells us introspection and consciousness are unreliable bases for self-knowledge. We know this is true but ignore it all the time. I'll do an hour of homework a day, not leave it to the end of vacation. If we adopt a dog, I'll walk it. If I buy a house, I'll be happy. I'll only have one drink. We are more than we think, as Walt Whitman wrote in *Song of Myself*.

> Do I contradict myself?

> Very well then I contradict myself

> (I am large, I contain multitudes.)

Our best laid plans go awry because complexity exists within as well as without. Our chaotic, intertwingled bodyminds are ecosystems inside ecosystems. No wonder it's hard to predict. Still, it's wise to seek self truth, or at least that's what I think.

Upon reflection, my mirror neurons tell me I'm a shy introvert who loves reading, hiking, and planning. I avoid conflict when possible but do not lack courage. Once I set a goal, I may focus and filter relentlessly. I embrace habit and eschew novelty. If I fail, I tend to pivot rather than persist. Who I am is changing. I believe it's speeding up. None of these traits is bad or good, as all things are double-edged. But mindful self awareness holds value. The more I notice the truth, the better my plans become.

Years ago, I planned a family vacation on St. Thomas. I kept it simple: a place near a beach where we could snorkel. It was a wonderful, relaxing escape. But over time a different message made it past my filters. Our girls had been bored. I dismissed it at first. I'd planned a shared experience I recalled fondly. It hurt to hear otherwise. But at last I did listen and learn. They longed not for escape but adventure. Thus our trip to Belize. I found planning and executing stressful due to risk, but I have no regrets. We shared a joyful adventure we'll never forget.

Way back when we were juggling toddlers, we accidentally threw out the mail. Bills went unpaid, notices came, we swore we'd do better, then lost mail again. One day I got home from work to find an indoor mailbox system made with paint cans. My wife Susan built it in a day. We've used it to sort and save mail for 15 years. It's an epic life hack I'd never have done. My ability to focus means I filter things out. I ignore problems and miss fixes. I'm not sure I'll change. Perhaps it merits a prayer.

> God grant me the serenity
> to accept the things I cannot change,
> courage to change the things I can,
> and wisdom to know the difference.

We also seek wisdom in others. This explains our fascination with the statistics of regret. End of life wishes often include:

> I wish I'd taken more risks, touched more lives, stood up to bullies, been a better spouse or parent or child. I should have followed my dreams, worked and worried less, listened more. If only I'd taken better care of myself, chosen meaningful work, had the courage to express my feelings, stayed in touch. I wish I'd let myself be happy.

While they do yield wisdom, last wishes are hard to hear. We are skeptics for good reason. Memory prepares for the future, and that too is the aim of regret. It's unwise to trust the clarity of rose-colored glasses. The memory of pain and anxiety fades in time, but our desire for integrity grows. When time is short, regret is a way to rectify. I've learned my lesson. I'm passing it on to you. I'm a better person now. Don't make my mistakes. It's easy to say "I wish I'd stood up to bullies," but hard to do at the time. There's wisdom in last wishes but bias and self-justification too. Confabulation means we edit memories with no intention to deceive. The truth is elusive. Reflection is hard.

Belief in Change

In *Liminal Thinking* Dave Gray states that "beliefs are often the main thing standing in the way of change,"[3] and illustrates his belief with a story. Once upon a time, Dave adopted a rescue dog named Spitfire. All was well until New Year's Eve when he gave the dog a bone and Spitfire turned evil. The dog began to growl, and as Dave's son tried to calm the wild dog, Spitfire bit him. Using his theory of mind, Dave thinks he knows why.

> The dog had a belief, a story, in his head. The story in his head probably was something like, if I get something good, I better protect it. Anyone who approaches me is trying to take it away.[4]

His story was no longer the truth. The territory had changed, but Spitfire had not updated his mental map. The dog's beliefs and behaviors were stuck in the past. Happily a dog whisperer helped old Spitfire learn new tricks, but that's another story.

Of course, we are stuck in the past all the time. History is the cradle of culture. We treasure old maps and rituals and resist change. We're also trapped by trauma. Bad experiences alter "the way the brain organizes information"[5] and leave us less able to "identify cause and effect, grasp long term effects of actions, or create coherent plans for the future."[6] Trauma yields "somatic symptoms for which no clear physical basis can be found,"[7] including chronic back pain, migraines, and fatigue. The truth hides in the body. Recovery requires learning to tell the truth, even if that truth is brutally painful, and self-awareness, which is why the cardinal phrases in trauma therapy are "Notice that" and "What happens next?"[8]

Did you notice the question that started the chapter? Asked by Alan Turing in 1950, it's intriguing still today. He reframed the problem as the "imitation game."[9] A computer that deceives a human into thinking it is human by using natural language is intelligent and able to think. We call his game the Turing test.

Now we see Alan was playing an imitation game of his own. A world class marathoner and father of artificial intelligence, he served England in World War II, cracked the Enigma code, cut short the war by two years, and saved 14 million lives. He is a hero who hid that he was gay. In 1952, his secret revealed, he was convicted of homosexuality and sentenced to chemical castration. After eating a cyanide-laced apple, Alan died at 41.

I was born in England less than 20 years later, and we moved to the United States when I was eight. Not until college did I know I knew a homosexual. But I knew and told cruel jokes. By grad school, I had changed. There was no pivotal argument or experience. I spent time with gay people, and gradually my lizard brain learned there's nothing to fear. My story is alien to our girls. Life in the openly diverse community of Ann Arbor made them fearless of LGBTQ+ early on. But I realize we live in a bubble. Bigotry is rife. It's illegal to be gay in 70 countries, and in several the penalty is death. Culture holds us back, but it's nature too. Our brains grasp the categories of us and them instinctually. Racism, sexism, ageism, classism, heterosexism, and xenophobia are prehistoric. Tribalism is as old as the hills.

People like and unlike Turing must play the imitation game. That's an uncomfortable fact of here and now. Progress isn't easy. We need to engage Systems 2 and 1. Science and reason only go so far. Intuition and emotion, like machine learning, are only as good as the data set. Exposure to diversity is key. But it begins with reflection. We won't fix what we don't see. Oscar Wilde says "the truth is rarely pure and never simple."[10] Yet if we dare to reflect in earnest, to admit we're not as good as we may think, we can make the map visible, and change it.

Alan asks "Can machines think?" I'm at least as interested in seeing if they can help us think and feel. The algorithms we're using to build companies, societies, and AIs are conventional and simplistic. The risks of artificial intelligence may be offset by intelligence augmentation; but we'll need compassion too.

Principles to Practices

All stars make light, but the spark of insight needs reflection. To be social, we might ask observers for feedback. What do you see in what I do that may change the way I am? Of course it's hard to tell and hear the truth. That's why in Japan, the roads from *tatamae* façade to *honne* truth are paved with saké.

To make reflection tangible, write to learn. Journal therapy is among the best ways to promote self-awareness and growth, and helps people face the truth of trauma. Or to change tack, sketch three alternative versions of the next five years of your life. Note a headline and hypothesis for each. Creating visual timelines or *Odyssey Plans* helps you look forward and back. [11]

For agile introspection, play *Start, Stop, Continue.*[12] Put a blank poster on the wall for each category. Take 15 minutes to write on sticky notes things from the last sprint to stop or continue and things for the next sprint to start. Next, sort similar notes into clumps. Dot voting to prioritize is optional. Discuss and reflect as a group, and close with decisions and action items.

But don't only reflect on sprints. Diverse increments generate singular insights. Plan ahead one year, look back two. Or for radical reflection, use a sunset review. Identify methods and deliverables to be abolished in the absence of action to renew.

To double down on reflecting, try the two hour rule. Block a two hour period weekly just to think. Balance usual questions with unstructured time to wonder. You have no idea where you might go. To change what you notice, choose a partner. Plan to share observations after meetings. What did you see?

What did I miss? Or write a letter to the future. The you that reads it may be surprised by what you wrote. Or meditate on the story of the farmer and his son. To every claim of good or bad luck, the farmer answers "maybe." Once upon a time, we played a game to ready our girls for life. Did it help? Are they well prepared? Maybe so. Maybe not. Or maybe we'll not see.

Star Finder

"I dream of a world guided by stories
rooted in the revelations of science and
framed with an indigenous worldview."
– ROBIN WALL KIMMERER

In the town where I belong, there's a well-trodden path. If you were to wander by, you might spy golden daffodils and a man who walks with a dog. Rest beside the path, beneath the trees, and you may wonder why the man now walks a different dog. What's up? Like an octopus with a coconut, you see an act but not the plan. Intent is but a fleeting glimpse of the inward eye.

We walk the path of this book, you and I, but as our adventure together nears its end, we don't know the other's intent. We've explored principles, practices, willpower, waypower, memory, myth, and the embodied design of paths and goals. But why?

What future do our acts predict? Is it fear or a way we hope to feel? What story do we tell to make it worthwhile? Who do we love? How do we help? What is the meaning of life? You and I have come too far to not go deep, but let's pivot for a pause.

Paths and Goals

My star finder is fixed by two sisters. Claire is the elder. She's a straight line like me. Claudia is the younger and as squiggly as her mom. Claire has grit for better and for worse. Claudia's a free spirit, as forgiving as forgetful. I love both and am truly grateful they are so different. Parallax hurts but it's also a gift.

Yet we must not fix on difference. The playful improviser and rigorous planner are not real. They are categories we invent to understand, but like all maps hide as much as reveal. We exist on infinite spectra. So I can't tell you how to plan. People and organizations may define paths and goals that limit liabilities and play to strengths. Difference is the essence of strategy. But competition is not the only way. Kindness and compassion are everything on the well-trodden path to joyful, meaningful life.

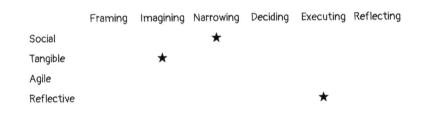

	Framing	Imagining	Narrowing	Deciding	Executing	Reflecting
Social			★			
Tangible		★				
Agile						
Reflective					★	

Figure 8-1. A star finder matrix.

You get to write your own story. Be a hero or helper, or define a new role. It's your choice. My hope is for you to succeed. The star finder matrix may help. Identify an intersection worthy of reconstruction, and on your next project, plan different. If your habit is to imagine and stop, make narrowing social to prevent procrastination. Fit paths to your context and personality, and you'll realise your goals, as where there's a way, there's a will.

Niccolò Machiavelli never wrote "the ends justify the means," but that's one way to interpret *The Prince*. Some see it as satire or a trick to undo tyranny. The author's intent is unknown, so we can't know if the plan worked. We do know he put a dent in the universe. Five centuries later we still debate his words, and we tend to construe history as a battle of means and ends.

Consider, for illustration, the tale of Joan of Arc. In 1412 when Joan was born, France seemed destined to control by England. At the age of thirteen, this peasant girl began to receive visions from God, often in the form of divinely specific instructions.

> I have been commanded to do two things on the part of the King of Heaven: one, to raise the siege of Orleans; the other, to conduct the King to Rheims for his sacrament and his coronation.[1]

Miraculously, at seventeen, Joan was put in charge of the army of France, achieved both her stated goals, and turned the tide of the Hundred Years' War. A year later, captured by England, she was burned at the stake for the heresy of cross-dressing. That she wore armor in battle to be safe and pants in prison to deter rape was no matter. Joan's trial was a means to an end.

Later, the Pope ordered a retrial, and Joan was canonized as a Roman Catholic Saint. Ultimately, even the English fell in love with the French heroine. Wordsworth named her "a perfect woman, nobly plann'd, to warn, to comfort, and command,"[2] and Churchill wrote "she finds no equal in a thousand years."

Mark Twain said "She was perhaps the only entirely unselfish person whose name has a place in profane history"[3] and wrote his best book on the story of her life. Oddly, his infatuation, in part, was due to his belief Joan uniquely embodied free will.

> For Twain the one person documented in the record of history whose actions were genuinely free, innocent, and devoid of selfishness was Joan of Arc. In no way, he believed, could her actions have been predicted or even now completely understood by applying with objectivity the norms of historical determinism.[4]

Joan inspired France and terrified England because her belief, "I have done nothing but by God's command," was shared by the people. It's odd Twain saw her as an angel of means and ends, yet ignored a planning hero who lived so close to home.

John Brown is best known for a failed raid on a federal armory at Harpers Ferry, but it's wrong to frame him as a bad planner. He endured terrible setbacks in life, yet embodied and advised resolve, "I wish you to have some definite plan. Many seem to have none; others never stick to any that they do form." He led men into war, but asked his children for input, "I want to plan with you a little; and I want you all to express your minds."[5]

His plan to end slavery in the United States had been forming and changing in shape from 1828 when he proposed to start a Negro school in Hudson until 1859 when he finally decided on Harpers Ferry. John worked with abolitionist leaders and the Underground Railroad, but grew convinced that violence was necessary. The armory was the first step in his plan to free and arm slaves, and engage in guerilla warfare. But he was undone by bad luck. Harriet Tubman helped plan the raid but fell sick and couldn't participate. And one of John's men let him down by not delivering a wagon of arms at a critical juncture. John was captured by Robert E. Lee, tried for treason, and hanged.

Figure 8-2. A curving path to intent.

John lived the Golden Rule, realized "the price of repression is greater than the cost of liberty,"[6] and had no desire to escape the consequences of his act. In fact, he was cheerful to the end, as he saw he may yet achieve his full intent, noting "I think I cannot now better serve the cause I love so much than to die for it; and in my death I may do more than in my life."[7]

Two decades later, Frederick Douglass said "if John Brown did not end the war that ended slavery, he did, at least, begin the war that ended slavery."[8] And fifty years after his violent act of transgression, W. E. B. Du Bois wrote "Only in time is truth revealed. Today at last we know: John Brown was right."

For contrast, let's reflect for a moment on the life of Gandhi, who led India to independence with a means of nonviolent civil disobedience named *satyagraha* or insistence on truth. He never said "be the change you wish to see," but he believed it.

> Your belief that there is no connection between the means and the end is a great mistake…there is just the same inviolable connection between the means and the end as between the seed and the tree.[9]

Gandhi refused to compromise his principles for any goal. He is celebrated as a hero but died feeling he'd failed. In the midst of several fasts unto death to stop religious violence, Gandhi was shot by a Hindu who thought him too kind to Muslims.

Mandela believed in "the right of every man to plan his own future,"[10] and although he held nonviolence as a core principle at first, he later saw force as the only means to end apartheid.

> Nonviolent passive resistance is effective as long as your opposition adheres to the same rules as you do. But if peaceful protest is met with violence, its efficacy is at an end.[11]

As chairman of MK or "spear of the nation" Nelson Mandela built and led the armed wing of the *African National Congress*.

> In planning the direction and form that MK would take, we considered four types of violent activities: sabotage, guerilla warfare, terrorism, and open revolution…it made sense to start with…sabotage…because it did not involve loss of life, it offered the best hope for reconciliation among the races afterward.[12]

Eventually, Mandela was arrested for sabotage and conspiracy to violently overthrow the government, and condemned to life imprisonment. After 27 years in prison, Mandela was released. He went on to end apartheid, and after being elected President of South Africa, created the *Truth and Reconciliation Commission* to deliver restorative justice, because Mandela never lost hope.

> I always knew that deep down in every heart, there is mercy and generosity. No one is born hating another because of the color of his skin, or his background, or his religion. People must learn to hate, and if they can learn to hate, they can be taught to love, for love comes more naturally to the human heart than its opposite.[13]

There is no one right way to be a hero. Each of these freedom fighters chose a singular means to an end, except for Joan who was led by God. All were highly principled and willing to die for a cause, but they had differing plans, beliefs, and values.

Figure 8-3. Union of path and goal.

In particular, faith in the bond of means and ends sets Gandhi apart. This belief traces back to the *Bhagavad Gita*, the ancient Hindu scripture that defines yoga as a union of path and goal.

> Self-possessed, resolute, act
>
> without any thought of results,
>
> Open to success or failure.
>
> This equanimity is yoga.[14]

While meditation bears understanding, the yoga of action is a direct path to serenity and wisdom. Gandhi explains "He who gives up action, falls. He who gives up only the reward, rises.

But renunciation of fruit in no way means indifference to the result." Yoga is deep, difficult to realise, yet vital to our future.

Organisms as Algorithms

Have you noticed old folks don't trust Google Maps? They are sure they know a better way. It's not only that our elders don't understand how it works, but also because they don't want to believe it's true. A consolation of age is that we know the way. We call it wisdom. And it hurts to be displaced by algorithms.

In *Homo Deus*, Yuval Noah Harari says "algorithm is arguably the single most important concept in our world."[15] He explores the history of belief from animism to theism to humanism, and explains the agricultural revolution gave rise to Gods, but then science made humans the source of all meaning and authority.

> For 300 years the world has been dominated by humanism, which sanctifies the life, happiness, and power of Homo sapiens.[16]

Noah writes history to shape the future, and frames us at the dawn of a titanic religious revolution fired by computers.

> Like capitalism, Dataism began as a neutral scientific theory, but is now mutating into a religion that claims to determine right and wrong. The supreme value of the new religion is *information flow*.[17]

In this myth, freedom of information is the greatest good. We must all do our part by sharing data. We are not important as individuals. Organisms are *algorithms* fed by data. Connecting to the system is the source of all meaning. We must relinquish authority to artificial intelligence, as it will know a better way.

I think Noah may be right about dataism, but I don't feel good about where we're going. It makes sense that as computers get smarter, we'll increasingly trust agents to plan our lives. Maps of roads and traffic flows are only the first step. Noah explains "humans are in danger of losing their economic value, because intelligence is decoupling from consciousness," and herein lies my unease. I fear we've taken a fork in the road, and I'd like to give it back. While civilization makes things to be grateful for, the system takes its toll by repressing what we feel and value.

Our steps trace back to Descartes who promoted intelligence over consciousness and classified animals as automata without minds or souls. *I think therefore I am* was a warrant for cruelty from vivisection in the 17th century to factory farming today.

Of course, there are others to blame. Two millennia ago, Ovid wrote the motto – *exitus acta probat* – on the coat of arms of George Washington that inspired the American flag. Under our stars and stripes, 9 million Native Americans died and 12.5 million Africans were enslaved. Did Ovid pave the way for slavery and genocide with "the result justifies the deed?"

In the face of sacrifice, it's dangerous yet vital to ask questions. What ends might justify such means? Some of us enjoy health and wealth, but complicity makes us unhappy. Corporations are algorithms that optimize for profit and demand insatiable growth. Our way of life is unfair and unsustainable. We are the agents of climate change and mass extinction. The leading cause of early death is pollution, and suicide is on the rise. As the villain-victim of cultural trauma, we can't handle the truth.

In the *Bhagavad Gita*, the hero Arjuna asks the god Krishna to reveal his Self, and then describes the terrifying vision he sees.

Your stupendous form, your billions

of eyes, limbs, bellies, mouths, dreadful

fangs: seeing them the worlds

tremble, and so do I.[18]

Upon detonating the first atom bomb, J. Robert Oppenheimer recalled Lord Krishna's response, "I am death, shatterer of worlds, annihilating all things."[19] Trauma is a natural reaction to our story, but we need not stay stuck. Truth is the first step.

I do not believe organisms are algorithms or that the ends will ever justify our meanness. In 1823, Jeremy Bentham wrote "the question is not, Can they reason? nor, Can they talk? but, Can they suffer?"[20] and I agree. We might plan a sustainable future, but if we walk a road of cruelty paved with us and them, we will never reach our goal. There are no externalities in a world that's *intertwingled*, and repression doesn't work. As we lose face to the superior algorithms of corporations and computers, our suffering may teach us to value consciousness over intelligence. Need we wait so long for kindness, compassion, and wisdom? Our children see the truth. I feel therefore I am.

Sentient Sanctuary

Do you remember those golden daffodils and the man who walks with dogs? If you stroll down the path, you'll see a sign for *Humane Society of Huron Valley* and guess what's going on. I'm a volunteer. Once a week, I walk a few dogs. On occasion, I feel fear upon entering the kennel of a 65 pound pit bull, but mostly I feel happy to walk and play with my spirited friends.

This story bares a green branch on my life path. I am not in the habit of help. I'm good to family and friends, but outside those concentric circles, I'm no more generous with time or money than the next guy. When I told Susan and the girls my plan to volunteer, they laughed and bet I'd last a couple of weeks. But a year later, I'm a faithful dog walker, and do not plan to stop.

For a quarter century, I've worked with organizations to plan software and websites. I love what I do, but in nearing the age of fifty, I also wonder what's next. For years, I suffered from a failure of the imagination. My childhood dreams were limited to being a soccer player and having a horse. As an adult, all I had was "maybe I'll teach." But insight came in time. Instead of planning the next few years, I decided to design Life Three.

If the first was education, and the second family plus career, how might I spend my third quarter century? This time frame opened my mind. I imagined a variety of possible futures, yet one calls out with spirit and depth as a vision I wish to share.

There's a place I call *Sentient Sanctuary* in a land of rivers, hills, meadows, and trees. On a summer's day, you may see folks seek shelter in the shade of a solar barn. Cats, dogs, chickens, horses; it's a little like Noah's ark. As a boy plays with a goat, and a girl with a robot, we all explore the meaning of *sentience*.

A sentient being is able to think or feel. All animals, including humans, are sentient. As subjects, not objects, we fear pain and desire pleasure. We bear memories, plans, and goals. Robots are not sentient yet, but that's a good question to ask. In the edges are the plants. Trees, for instance, have plans.[21] Acacias use ethylene gas to warn neighbors of hungry giraffes. Mother beech trees use root systems to pass sugar to hungry children. Oaks plan together for acorns years in advance. We're unsure how much plants think or feel. I predict we have a lot to learn.

Gandhi believed Ahimsa. This principle of nonviolence in word or deed applies to all living beings. He also understood to do no harm is impossible. We all suffer and cause suffering. It's the fearful truth of life. But if we accept our responsibility and act with compassion, we may yet discover joy and wonder in the diversity of sentience, and its universality too.

The sanctuary is a refuge from and for change. Folks may visit for an hour or a week for tours, classes, conferences, meals, art, concerts, and experiments. It's a sacred space to plan together, so I can't know yet what it might become. Perhaps you will be there one day to listen, unlearn, and speak new myths. I write of it now so that you may help in a way only you know how.

In *Braiding Sweetgrass* Robin Wall Kimmerer tells a lovely story in a chapter on collateral damage about saving salamanders in upstate New York. Once a year, en masse, in the dark of night, black and yellow amphibians, seven inches long, migrate from burrows to ponds. So, flashlights in hands, Robin and her daughter spend hours together helping them cross the road. It's like the fable of the boy who throws starfish back into the ocean, but with a potent twist. As a citizen and student of the Potawatomi and a professor of environmental biology, Robin uses indigenous wisdom and science to look for levers. She imagines culverts to channel salamanders beneath the road, and writes a story to engage us in reciprocity and gratitude.

> What crazy species leaves a warm home on a rainy night to ferry salamanders across the road? It's tempting to call it altruism, but it's not. There is nothing selfless about it. This night rewards the givers as well as the recipients. We get to be there, to witness this amazing rite, and, for an evening, to enter into relationship with other beings, as different from ourselves as we can imagine.[22]

This is my hope for *Sentient Sanctuary*. I wish to create a small place of happiness with the potential to make a big difference. My dream lives in the union of path and goal. I don't know I'll get there. It will take time to think and feel my way into who I am as a helper. So I walk with dogs on a well-trodden path.

Organizing the Future

In the story of Noah's ark, elephants are safely aboard, yet in the last hundred years, we have reduced them by 99 percent. Our lust for ivory is a problem, but so are roads and farms.

> To survive now, many elephants must abandon exactly the learned traditions and knowledge – the cultures – that have kept them alive: ancient migration routes, and centuries old, handed down paths to known reserves of food and water, reserves that themselves are vanishing as people occupy and replace them.[23]

In an era of disruption, isn't this our problem too? As cultures shift, traditions lose meaning, wisdom loses value, and we lose our way. Uncertainty, chaos, and disinformation challenge our will to plan. But despair makes trauma worse. We will answer with truth and hope. The truth hurts yet we can handle it, and even the tallest mountains are no match for our shared mix of willpower and waypower. While sanctuary offers time to rest, I'm at my best when on a quest. Is adventure the way for you?

You are the hero. You write your story. You design your paths and goals. Mindset is key. A baby elephant, who learns a rope binds her leg to a tree, grows into an adult who's trapped only by her mind. A hero is shaped by culture yet not repressed by laws and norms. In my town live two people from Nepal who made a secret plan. They fell in love but were forbidden to be together due to different faiths, one Buddhist, one Hindu. So they escaped to the summit of Mount Everest, removed their oxygen masks, and held a wedding ceremony on the world's tallest peak.[24] Freedom may terrify us, but we can decide to be curious and go towards the fear. A mountain isn't everyone's cup of tea, but that's the joy of waymaking. You get to choose your own adventure, even if there is no path. There's wisdom in humility, as in every belief is a lie, but it also makes sense to feel hope. There's so much good to discover. As a wise man once wrote "the future isn't just unwritten – it's unsearched."[25]

The lady who loves to save salamanders also hopes to save us. In braiding a sweetgrass of science and wisdom, Robin shares her vision of mutual flourishing and suggests it's not too late.

> In indigenous ways of knowing, time is not a river, but a lake in which the past, present, and future exist. Creation is an ongoing process and the story is not history alone; it is also prophecy.[26]

In the teachings of her ancestors, responsibilities and gifts are but two sides of a coin. At the heart of her culture of gratitude is the principle of reciprocity. We should give thanks to the plants and animals for food, clothing, shelter, and to the stars for guiding us home, yet we must also give back to the Earth.

> The most important thing each of us can know is our unique gift and how to use it in the world. Individuality is cherished and nurtured, because, in order for the whole to flourish, each of us has to be strong in who we are and carry our gifts with conviction.[27]

One way to discover your unique gift is through the design of paths and goals. Traditional habits and beliefs settle our lives, but planning for everything opens the door to change. By the title, I mean three things. First, planning is a flexible skill we can use in any context. Second, we must plan to improvise, as surprise is inevitable. Third, I hope we plan for consequence and the second to third order impact of our actions on others.

Figure 8-4. Planning for everything.

My plan nears its end. I'm out of words. It is time to pass the spark. You are a star finder. You design your paths and goals. You get the freedom to plan and let go. I hope our paths cross. I wish you luck. In search of new stories, I ask you questions.

Tell me, what else should I have done?

Doesn't everything die at last, and too soon?

Tell me, what is it you plan to do

with your one wild and precious life?[28]

Afterword

I wrote this book to help everyone on the full spectrum from playful improviser to rigorous planner to become better at the design of paths and goals. Now you've read it, I can use your help. Will you spread the word? To make a big splash, write a review on **Amazon**. A sentence or two with a handful of stars is a gift that makes a difference. Of course, there's no one right way to help, so whatever you plan, let me simply say **thanks**.

And if you're not tired of me yet and hope to get in touch, I'm easily findable at **intertwingled.org** and **semanticstudios.com**. If you believe there might be a fit between your needs and my **planning services** as a speaker, consultant, or coach, let's talk.

Notes

Chapter 1, Realising the Future

[1] The Fourfold Way: Peter Morville Interviews Rachel Joyce (2016).

[2] Attributed to Winston Churchill, yet appears to be apocryphal, which means of doubtful authenticity, although widely circulated as being true.

[3] Quoted in Six Crises (1962) by Richard Nixon.

[4] Cognitive Planning by J. P. Das, Binod C. Kar, Rauno K. Parrila (1996), p.34.

[5] Initial and Concurrent Planning in Solutions to Well-Structured Problems by Simon P. Davies (2003).

[6] The Intelligent Use of Space by David Kirsh (1995).

[7] Blueprints for Thinking by Sarah Friedman, Ellin Scholnick, Rodney Cocking (1987), p.217-224.

[8] Smarter, Faster, Better by Charles Duhigg (2017), p.23.

[9] Duhigg (2017), p.30.

[10] Hillbilly Elegy by J. D. Vance (2016), p.181.

[11] Getting Things Done by David Allen (2001).

[12] On Wit and Humour by William Hazlitt (1818).

[13] The Soul of an Octopus by Sy Montgomery (2016), p.82.

[14] Beyond Words: What Animals Think and Feel by Carl Safina (2015).

[15] Montgomery (2016), p.224.

[16] Montgomery (2016), p.115.

[17] Following the Equator by Mark Twain (1897), p.135.

[18] A Proposal for the Dartmouth Summer Research Project on Artificial Intelligence (1955).

[19] The Shape of Automation for Men and Management by Herbert Simon (1965), p.96.

[20] Marvin Minsky in Life Magazine (1970).

[21] Plans and Situated Actions by Lucy Suchman (1987), p.vii.

[22] Suchman (1987), p.27.

[23] Suchman (1987), p.26.

[24] Intelligence Without Representation by Rodney Brooks (1987).

[25] Brooks (1987).

[26] AlphaGo by David Silver and Demis Hassabis (2016).

[27] When Will AI Exceed Human Performance? by Katja Grace et. al. (2017).

[28] Artificial Intelligence is a Tool, not a Threat by Rodney Brooks (2014).

[29] Apocryphal, and may be Danish in origin.

[30] On Intelligence by Jeff Hawkins and Sandra Blakeslee (2005), p.86.

[31] Homo Prospectus by Martin Seligman et. al. (2016), p.x.

[32] Thinking Fast and Slow by Daniel Kahneman (2011).

[33] Seligman (2016), p.210.

[34] Seligman (2016), p.103.

[35] Adapted from Peter Morville's foreword to Understanding Context: Environment, Language, and Information Architecture by Andrew Hinton (2014).

[36] Seligman (2016), p.244.

[37] The Principles of Scientific Management by Frederick W. Taylor (1911).

[38] Management: Tasks, Responsibilities, Practices by Peter Drucker (1974), p.181.

[39] The One Best Way by Robert Kanigel (1997), p.372.

[40] The Machine That Changed the World by James Womack (1990), p.56.

[41] The Lean Startup by Eric Ries (2011).

[42] Learning Agile by Andrew Stellman and Jennifer Greene (2015), p.47.

[43] Strategy Safari by Henry Mintzberg, Bruce Ahlstrand, Joseph Lampel (1998), p.64.

[44] Quoted in The Guts of a New Machine, New York Times Magazine (2003).

[45] The Design Process: What is the Double Diamond? by the British Design Council (2015).

[46] I Am Malala by Malala Yousafzai with Christina Lamb (2013), p.310.

[47] He Named Me Malala by Malala Yousafzai and Davis Guggenheim (2015).

[48] Speech by Malala Yousafzai to the United Nations General Assembly (2013).

[49] Self-Reliance by Ralph Waldo Emerson (1841).

Chapter 2, Framing

[1] Marine Corps Planning Process, MCWP 5-1 (2010).

[2] Built to Last: Successful Habits of Visionary Companies by Jim Collins and Jerry Porras (1994).

[3] Walt Disney: Magician of the Movies by Bob Thomas (1966), p.116.

[4] How to Be Like Walt: Capturing the Disney Magic by Pat Williams (2004), p.69.

[5] The New Economics for Industry, Government, Education by W. Edwards Deming (2000), p.35.

[6] Goals Gone Wild by Lisa D. Ordóñez et. al. (2009).

[7] Ambient Findability: What We Find Changes Who We Become by Peter Morville (2005), p.162.

[8] The Art of Fear by Kristen Ulmer (2017), p.235.

[9] Rhetoric by Aristotle (350 BCE).

[10] Don't Think of an Elephant by George Lakoff (2004), p.xv.

[11] Words of Kat King (published with permission).

[12] Words of Richard Nixon during a press conference (1973).

[13] Influence: The Psychology of Persuasion by Robert Cialdini (1984), p.4-5.

[14] Speech by Steve Jobs at the World Wide Developers Conference (1997).

[15] The Battle for the Life and Beauty of the Earth by Christopher Alexander (2012), p.119.

[16] The Everything Store: Jeff Bezos and the Age of Amazon (2014).

[17] Jobs To Be Done: Theory to Practice by Anthony W. Ulwick (2016).

[18] When Things Fall Apart: Heart Advice for Difficult Times by Pema Chödrön (1996), p.2.

Chapter 3, Imagining

[1] The Psychology of Hope by C.R. Snyder (1994), p.11-12.

[2] Snyder (1994), p.12.

[3] Snyder (1994), p.8.

[4] Make It Stick by Peter C. Brown et. al. (2014). The statistics in this section are drawn directly from the book. The mnemonic is an adaptation based on ideas in the book.

[5] Made To Stick by Chip Heath and Dan Heath (2007), p.109.

[6] Helping by Edgar Schein (2009), p.2.

[7] Making Learning Whole by David Perkins (2010), p.49.

[8] Perkins (2010), p.51.

[9] Perkins (2010), p.76.

[10] Intertwingled by Peter Morville (2014), p.72.

[11] The Philosophy of the Handheld by Leander Kahney, Wired (1999).

[12] The Black Swan by Nassim Nicholas Taleb (2007), p.135.

[13] Before Europeans traveled to Australia, they believed all swans were white. A single black swan sighting invalidated thousands of years of empirical evidence.

[14] Antifragile by Nassim Nicholas Taleb (2012), p.173-174.

[15] The Power of Positive Deviance by Richard Pascale et. al. (2010).

[16] Gamestorming by Dave Gray, Sunni Brown, James Macanufo (2010).

[17] Adapted from a story in Intertwingled by Peter Morville (2014).

[18] Marine Corps Planning Process, MCWP 5-1 (2010).

[19] Bright Lights, No City by Max Alexander (2012), p.26.

[20] Thinking in Pictures by Temple Grandin (2006), p.11.

[21] Human, All Too Human by Friedrich Nietzsche (1880), p.360.

Chapter 4, Narrowing

[1] The Cognitive Psychology of Planning by Robin Morris and Geoff Ward (2005), p.64.

[2] For the full story, see Intertwingled by Peter Morville (2014).

[3] Living in Information: Architecture for Life Inside Small Glass Rectangles by Jorge Arango (2018).

[4] Intuitive Prediction by Daniel Kahneman and Amos Tversky (1979).

[5] If you disagree with this plan, remember: there's no one right way to make breakfast.

[6] Risk Savvy by Gerd Gigerenzer (2014), p.110.

[7] The Black Swan by Nassim Taleb (2007), p.211.

[8] Niels Bohr: His Life and Work by Hans Bohr (1967).

[9] The Paradox of Choice by Barry Schwartz (2004), p.3.

Chapter 5, Deciding

[1] Models of Man by Herbert Simon (1957).

[2] Prospect Theory by Daniel Kahneman and Amos Tversky (1979).

[3] Run Less, Run Faster by Bill Pierce, Scott Murr, and Ray Moss (2012).

[4] How Life Imitates Chess by Garry Kasparov (2007), p.80.

[5] Stop Worrying About Making the Right Decision by Ed Batista (2013).

[6] The Lean Startup by Eric Ries (2011), p.57.

[7] Follow the Yellow Brick Road by Richard Saul Wurman (1992), p.184.

[8] Marine Corps Planning Process, MCWP 5-1 (2010).

[9] We Shall Fight on the Beaches by Winston Churchill (1940).

Chapter 6, Executing

[1] The Lean Startup by Eric Ries (2011), p.77.

[2] Peace is Every Step by Thich Nhat Hanh (1991), p.35.

[3] Team of Teams by Stanley McChrystal (2015), p.59.

[4] McChrystal (2015), p.141.

[5] McChrystal (2015), p.163-164.

[6] Sources of Power: How People Make Decisions by Gary Klein (1999).

[7] Seeing What Others Don't by Gary Klein (2013), p.27.

[8] Grit: The Power of Passion and Perseverance by Angela Duckworth (2016), p.203.

[9] Duckworth (2016), p.202.

[10] Harriet Tubman: The Moses of Her People by Sarah Bradford (1886), p.17.

[11] Bradford (1886), p.60.

[12] Bradford (1886), p.41.

[13] Attributed to Leonard Bernstein, this quote appears to be apocryphal.

Chapter 7, Reflecting

[1] Make It Stick by Peter Brown et. al. (2014), p.133.

[2] Why You Don't Know Your Own Mind by Alex Rosenberg (2016).

[3] Liminal Thinking by Dave Gray (2016), p.xvi.

[4] Gray (2016), p.24.

[5] The Body Keeps the Score by Bessel Van Der Kolk (2014), p.3.

[6] Bessel Van Der Kolk (2014), p.45.

[7] Bessel Van Der Kolk (2014), p.100.

[8] Bessel Van Der Kolk (2014), p.210.

[9] Computing Machinery and Intelligence by Alan Turing (1950).

[10] The Importance of Being Earnest by Oscar Wilde (1895).

[11] Designing Your Life by Bill Burnett and Dave Evans (2016), p.96.

[12] Apps by Retrium, http://retrium.com.

Chapter 8, Star Finder

[1] Speech by Joan of Arc to her knights on the road to Chinon (1429).

[2] A Phantom of Delight by William Wordsworth (1804).

[3] Joan of Arc by Mark Twain (1896), p.20.

[4] Twain (1896), p.15.

[5] John Brown by W. E. B. Du Bois (1909), p.62.

[6] Du Bois (1909), p.4.

[7] Du Bois (1909), p.213.

[8] Du Bois (1909), p.211.

[9] Nonviolent Resistance (Satyagraha) by M. K. Gandhi (1961), p.10.

[10] Long Walk to Freedom by Nelson Mandela (1994), p.85.

[11] Mandela (1994), p.158.

[12] Mandela (1994), p.282.

[13] Mandela (1994), p.622.

[14] Bhagavad Gita, translation by Stephen Mitchell (2002), p.55.

[15] Homo Deus by Yuval Noah Harari (2017), p.83.

[16] Harari (2017), p.65.

[17] Harari (2017), p.386.

[18] Mitchell (2002), p.136.

[19] Mitchell (2002), p.138.

[20] Introduction to the Principles of Morals and Legislation by Jeremy Bentham (1789).

[21] The Hidden Life of Trees by Peter Wohlleben (2015).

[22] Braiding Sweetgrass by Robin Wall Kimmerer (2013), p.358.

[23] Beyond Words: What Animals Think and Feel by Carl Safina (2016), p.67.

[24] Wedding on Top of Mount Everest, BBC News (2005).

[25] Quote by Bruce Sterling in Ambient Findability by Peter Morville (2005).

[26] Kimmerer (2013), p.343.

[27] Kimmerer (2013), p.134.

[28] The Summer Day by Mary Oliver (1992).

Index

About the Author

Peter Morville has been helping people and organizations to plan since 1994. Clients include AT&T, Cisco, Harvard, IBM, the Library of Congress, Macy's, Microsoft, Tufts University, the National Cancer Institute, and Vodafone. Books include *Information Architecture*, *Ambient Findability*, *Search Patterns*, and *Intertwingled*. He has delivered conference keynotes and workshops in North America, South America, Europe, Asia, and Australia. His work has appeared in *The Economist*, *NPR*, and *The Wall Street Journal*. Peter plans in Ann Arbor with his wife, two daughters, and a wicked smart dog named *Knowsy*.

42383835R00080

Made in the USA
Middletown, DE
16 April 2019